BIOGRAPHY OF A RIVER

BIOGRAPHY
OF A RIVER

THE PEOPLE AND LEGENDS
OF THE HUDSON VALLEY

by John Mylod

Alec Thomas: *Editor*

BONANZA BOOKS · NEW YORK

0-517-L0208X
Copyright © MCMLXIX by Auric Arts Film Productions, Inc.
Library Of Congress Catalog Card Number: 78-85437
All rights reserved.
This edition is published by Bonanza Books
a division of Crown Publishers, Inc.
by arrangement with Hawthorn Books
a b c d e f g h
Manufactured in the United States of America

Photographs, unless otherwise credited, are by Robert Greene.

Credit for the chapter opening illustrations on pages 49 and 69 goes to the New York Public Library.

Design: Harold Franklin

To my father
—J.M.

To my Princess Rosanne and my
bandits, Michael and Stuart
—A.T.

It is a great pleasure to acknowledge here the help and encouragement of many people who guided me in the preparation of this manuscript.

I should like very much to especially thank Miss Allison Withers for her patience and generous assistance in the organization of the text.

I can hardly thank the members of my family enough for their endurance, and Mr. John J. Dworak—sportsman, photographer, and poet—who was forced to listen for long hours to the research material.

In addition, I am grateful to Mrs. Benjamin S. Hayden, Miss Mary V. Mylod, Miss Audrey Bynoe, Mrs. Elizabeth Blair, Mr. Joseph Cassidy, Miss Audrey Ann Bohlen-Gibbs, Mr. and Mrs. Hobart M. Brockway, the Penn Central Railroad, Mr. H. B. Berkshire, of the Penn Central, Miss Estelle Whelan, and Mrs. Michael Conkey for tolerating my persistence.

I wish also to thank the Mobil Oil Corporation, especially Captain T. Fender, Captain James Costello, Mr. William Happ, Captain Jurgen Johnson, and the crewmen of *Mobil 9* for their immediate and generous cooperation.

J.M.
Poughkeepsie

Ships,
All and any kind of water craft converging
On the River,
On the Hudson,
Flying the flags of the United Nations,
Harbor bound and sea bound,
Caught up in the blear and smear of trade and travel. Boats!
Boats,
Twenty thousand horses' power, harnessed,
Drawing teams of sand barges like a sow and her brood—
Contraband falls over the side of the *Rusty Maru*
A Chevrolet nearly drives off the end of the Staten Island Ferry
Small boats, boats you would hardly think floatable,
Swirling, almost capsizing, capsizing in Hell's Gate
Under the bridge, under the Boston to Washington express—
Swerving in the Kill Van Kull
Tankers,
The big guys, two football fields long measured on end,
Superships,
SS United States,
QE 2,
Long,
(Almost as long as the Empire State Building on its side)

Bending around the knuckle at the 44th Street pier because
Longshoremenareonstrike.
Bottoms,
Foreign registry, some ours, some theirs,
Inbound, quarantined, hats from Guyana, Guyana?
Unloading, loading
Minidresses for pygmy villages in Alabama,
Cadavers for Khartoum,
Container ships, carrying wholefreighttrains,
See the Statue of Liberty ships,
Ships towed,
Towing boats,
Snubnosed in the ferry's wash,
Allison Moran,
Catamaran,
Trimaran,
Classes—
Classless—
Seaworthyless—
Sailing—
Ships,
Ships,
Ships,
Ships,
Ships . . .

—J. M.

BIOGRAPHY
OF A RIVER

ONE

THE HUDSON has endured civilization. These days we usually destroy in a generation what Nature has spent millennia putting together; yet, considering its potential, the Hudson has not suffered grievously. There is now a powerful emphasis on maintaining public control of scenic, historic, and wilderness areas to protect the river and the people of its corridor against indiscriminate profit taking. Measures have been taken to correct damage already done to the river. Men have legislated to preserve the vast humanizing resources of the Hudson and its valley, but this is only part of a paradox.

For fully half its length the Hudson is not a river at all but an arm of the Atlantic, carried by tides to Troy and the mouth of the Mohawk. From there to the sea these undulating tides have been flowing inland and out at regular intervals for thousands of years. At Troy, where the river's floor begins to climb above sea level, the fresh water flows of the Mohawk and upper Hudson halt the penetrating flood thrust of the ocean. Tidewater Hudson is a remarkably straight river of lakes, connected by ribbons of water between pinched shorelines, and deep enough to accommodate salt-water shipping.

A few thousand years before Dutch fur trappers first built sod huts on Manhattan Island early in the seventeenth century, men of a far different tradition came to live along the shores of the Hudson River. They were of a people called Algonquians who followed land routes from as far west as the Pacific and traveled cross-country in a migratory procession that American pioneers reversed during the eighteenth and nineteenth centuries. It is uncertain just when these people began the trek eastward but, according to an ancient Indian prophecy, conveyed to each new generation by crude drawings and aboriginal dances, their nomadic journey would end in prosperity and peace when they discovered a great stream with "water that flows two ways." After long years of wandering that eventually brought them across central New York State and through the Mohawk valley, the Algonquians finally reached the great stream of the prophecy—the Hudson. From there they spread south along the tidewater from the Albany region and settled in a loosely organized brotherhood of tribes.

The Mohicans, "people of the water that flows two ways," were the strongest of all Algonquian tribes along the river. Their territory extended north from the present capital district to the region above Lake George. South of Mohican territory the Wappingers and Manhattans lived in peace along the river's eastern shore. On the western bank were tribes belonging to the Lenape union. Among them were the Wawarsings, Catskills, Haverstraws, Tappans, Hackensacks, and Raritans.

The wealth that these Indians found in the Hudson's valley was abundant. Animals for food and clothing were everywhere, and in the river striped bass, herring, sturgeon, and shad swam in overwhelming numbers. Archeological evidence also suggests that nearly 2,000 years before the Dutch settled on Manhattan, Indians ate oysters from the shallows of Newburgh and Haverstraw bays. Necklaces of rolled copper beads dating from the same period were found at a river site near the Greene County township of Catskill and suggest that these early Indians had attained more than a primeval level of development. Gradually, however, their war weapons became dull, and, as peaceful hunters, the Hudson River Indians were raided with impunity by Mohawks, Senecas, Oneidas, Cayugas, or

Onondagas, all members of the Iroquois federation. These tribes normally stayed within their own territory, the Finger Lake region of the state and the valleys of the Mohawk and Genesee rivers. But, whenever hardship threatened, they knew that they could always take from the weaker Algonquian people.

The Iroquois, however, were not interested in permanent settlements along the Hudson but looked to the river for food and for manpower to enslave. In later years the Dutch thought of the river in terms of furs, farms, patroons, and sailors' reaches. In 1664 the Duke of York could no longer resist the river's wealth or Dutch vulnerability and, claiming rightful ownership based on the earlier discoveries of John Cabot and John Smith, sent five ships, which seized the Netherlanders' land. During the American Revolution English generals considered control of the Hudson essential to a "divide and conquer" strategy that would quell the rebellion. After the war the Fulton steamboat and construction of the New York State barge canals inaugurated the river's great period of commercial growth. And twentieth-century engineers see it as a seam of water that they have tried to lace together below Albany with a dozen bridges.

Henry Hudson never did discover a shortcut to China and its treasures, but his third voyage in search of a clear passage around America, sponsored by the Dutch East India Company in 1609, brought him to the mouth of what he called the Great River of the Mountains. He did not give the river its present name. Mannahatta, Shatemuc, Cohatatea, Mahicanituk, and other Indian names confused the Dutch, who called the river Mauritius after their own Prince Maurice. After the English had, without bloodshed, captured the Dutch settlements clustered on the banks of the Mauritius they changed its name to Hudson's River. But practical boatmen and navigation charts in those early years called it North River to distinguish it from the Delaware to the south and the Connecticut to the east. Shippers still refer to the lowest quarter of the Hudson as North River.

On a map the river and its valley reflect a conglomeration of cultural threads. Shreds of Indian, Dutch, English, French, and German cultures remain in the names of cities, towns, roads, and local reference points throughout the Hudson's valley. Respect, pride, tradition, logic, and at times lack of imagination account for many place names along the river. North River, Glens Falls, Hudson Falls, Fort Edward, Schuylerville, Saratoga Springs, Stillwater, Mechanicville, Rensselaer, Grapeville, Coeymans, Stuyvesant, Hudson, Athens, New Baltimore, Cementon, West Camp, Saugerties, Tivoli, Kingston, Port Ewen, Hyde Park, Poughkeepsie, Wappingers Falls, New Hamburg, Chelsea, Newburgh, Beacon, Cold Spring, Manitou, Fort Montgomery, Tomkins Cove, Peekskill, Buchanan, Stony Point, Verplancks Point, Irvington, Dobbs Ferry, Hoboken, and Sandy Hook are just a sampling of the towns and tourist stops that continue as part of contemporary life. Through remaining evidence, myth, and memory we are able to maintain contact with the men and women who fashioned the river's present; we have inherited much more than place names on a map.

From its earliest recorded discovery by white men, the Hudson has been evaluated in terms of its commercial viability. The Florentine navigator Giovanni Verrazano found the river in 1524 but reported to King Francis I of France, for whom he sailed, that he had not penetrated much farther than the Narrows and Upper Bay, which he later described as "a beautiful lake." Verrazano touched only the tip of the Hudson's tongue and did not take the initiative for more extensive exploration. He was, nevertheless, aware of the river's potential. Leaving his ship *Dauphine* in Lower Bay he had discovered a "very agreeable situation" and recognized that the stream into which he sailed was "a very great river deep within the mouth which any laden ship might have passed." He had measured the tides at eight feet and knew that ships could navigate well here. What is interesting—and somewhat perplexing—is that he did not sail toward the upper Hudson. But caution may have been the navigator's style, and an unfavorable change in winds that forced his longboat back to the *Dauphine* probably discouraged further investigation. Very likely not wishing to endanger his ship or to communicate further with the natives, Verrazano, after only a short time on the river, bobbed along the coast of Long Island and eventually returned to Dieppe.

The summer of 1609 was over when Henry Hudson steered the tiny *Half Moon* into Upper Bay and headed toward the river's source. He and his crew were also cautious but less peaceful. After three weeks on the river they sailed for Holland leaving one crewman and several Indians dead in the September sun. While anchored near the western end of Long Island before starting up the river, Hudson was careful not to let on board his ship all the Indians who had rowed out to investigate the unusual sailing vessel and its even stranger crewmen. They came again to the *Half Moon,* bringing beans and oysters to trade, and impressed the Europeans with tobacco pipes of "yellow copper." Ship's mate Robert Juet, who jotted down details for a journal on Hudson's voyage, noted that "the river is full of fish" and that along its banks were "very loving people and very old men."

All along the river Hudson traded trifles for food and went on shore in the Catskill-Kinderhook region to visit some natives in their village. He brought an older Indian back aboard ship to find out how unruly he would be drunk but discovered that strong drink had a tendency to make the fellow somewhat talkative.

Hudson was, no doubt, disappointed when the shallow waters of the Middle Grounds above Kingston betrayed the promise of Haverstraw Bay's great width and the deep, though narrow, passage through the Highlands. At the end of September he hove to near Albany and sent a longboat ahead to take soundings. The boat returned with an unfavorable report, and, after concluding that navigation was impossible above Waterford, Hudson took careful notes on the wildlife and surrounding forests before dropping downriver. On September 29 he sailed the Long Reach from Crum Elbow past Poughkeepsie to where the Wappingers Creek cuts a furrow into the riverbed. There he anchored and ate. Indians came out to the ship but were afraid to board. A short time later more Indians paddled their crude dugout canoes to the sides of the *Half Moon* and Hudson traded for grain, "which we bought for trifles."

In the evening he sailed across Newburgh Bay but anchored in the lee of Storm King mountain instead of chancing a windy run through the Highlands. Robert Juet noted that Newburgh Bay offered suitable anchorage and thought it "a very good place for all winds save the east-north-east wind." Looking up past Pollepel Island he saw the rugged, wind-blasted face of Breakneck Mountain, nearly barren of trees. It appeared to Juet to have some minerals in the rock, suggesting that there might be riches there after all. Directly opposite Breakneck Mountain, Storm King Mountain presented the same possibilities, which did not go unnoticed.

From the Highlands to the Atlantic, Hudson did not have smooth going. One Indian, more ignorant than brave, shadowed the *Half Moon* until he found an appropriate opportunity to climb into a cabin. After stealing some gaudy clothing he was shot while trying to escape. When a boat was put over the side to retrieve the wardrobe, more redmen appeared. Foul language and gunfire sounded in the somnolent surroundings of Haverstraw Bay. One Indian drowned after his hands were cut off when he tried to overturn the small boat. There were more attacks on the ship. A whole party of bowmen gathered at Croton Point to strike at Hudson, but their attempt was futile, and the *Half Moon* headed toward the Narrows for the return trip to the Netherlands.

Hudson had again failed to bring back positive proof of a waterway west, but his reports concerning the Great River of the Mountains offered some cause for hope. Furs were abundant, he said, and the Indians had rich fields for wheat and corn. Unimpressed by Hudson's report, however, the Dutch were slow to investigate.

Samuel de Champlain had missed Hudson—and the river—by a month and by less than 100 miles. But French fur trappers soon followed his route into the lake region near Ticonderoga. It was not until 1613 that two Dutch captains, Hendrick Christiaenson and Adriaen Block, sailed in tandem to the Hudson and eventually reached Castle Island south of Albany, where they wintered in a hastily built palisade that they called Fort Nassau. In the following year a trading post was built on the Rondout Creek, and gradually more and more settlers came to the river valley. In a few years Fort Nassau was abandoned for a better position on higher ground, and the new stockaded trading village was called Fort Orange. More ships came. Eight, twelve, then eighteen families, many of them Walloon refugees from Holland, moved in to farm the land around Fort Orange before they eventually scattered to Esopus, Manhattan, Brooklyn, and Long Island. The traders who followed the early navigators and the settlers who began farming the valley during the middle quarter of the seventeenth century could not have functioned without the river. The powerful and compelling Hudson inspired fear and love in the early inhabitants who remained by its shores. Hudson's River provided food, communication, transportation, protection from Indians and wild animals, amusement, and beauty. Before long it began to work for them, providing power to turn mills and irrigation for crop land. Face to face with the river, men met its challenge and, of course, yielded to its fury. Most of all they sought its wealth.

The most ambitious colonization plan began in New Netherlands after 1629, when the government-monopolized Dutch West India Company, hoping to stimulate immigration and encourage growth of its chain of river trading posts into a permanent provincial establishment, issued the Charter of Privileges and Exemptions. The charter provided special privileges, including hereditary ownership, to any West India Company stockholder who would support at his own expense the settlement of at least fifty people on a tract of land over a four-year period. The only part of New Netherlands that the company reserved for itself was Manhattan. The men to whom the rights and responsibilities for these estates adhered were known as "patroons." With permission of the Director and Council of New Netherlands, nonshareholders, called "free colonists," could settle as much land as they could improve but without the powers and hereditary privileges that went with patroonship.

The river was the colonists' life blood, but spheres of exploration and settlement eventually began to extend inland. Ships transporting families and livestock were arriving in Upper Bay with increased frequency. They often landed first at Governors Island, where the people and their animals could become acclimated before being rowed across the mouth of the East River to Manhattan. Settling in both Albany and Manhattan at approximately the same time, Dutch farmers *(boers)* gradually started filling in the middle districts. Bolder men struck inland from the relative security of the Hudson settlements to occupy and improve the rich bottom land in Westchester, Dutchess, Columbia, Rensselaer, and Albany Counties. The forests were uncut, and Indian trails, although perilous, were the only overland routes available to the first landowners.

When DeVries sailed up the Hudson in 1640, formal organization of the independent village of Beverwyck (Albany) was twelve years away and of Wiltwyck (Kingston) thirteen. Walloons moved into New Platz in 1677, and by 1680 crops were being harvested in the valley of Kinderhook Creek, in Columbia County. Ten years before the turn of the eighteenth century a half-dozen men began to reclaim forest land at Poughkeepsie, and enough Dutchmen had settled in the Tarrytown region by 1699 to warrant a church at Sleepy Hollow.

Populating the Hudson valley was not a rapid process, nor was it limited to Dutchmen. From the time that Christiaenson and Block had first wintered at Castle Island, Dutch, Norwegian, Swedish, Flemish, French, German, and English adventurers had begun to arrive in the valley of the Hudson seeking substance in the land. In 1667 the population of New York was officially estimated to be about 8,000 settlers, but just before the Revolution a little more than 100 years later the total had risen to 168,038, including 18,883 blacks, practically all of whom were slaves.

If a farmer could protect his family and livestock from the first winter and the attacks of bears, wildcats, wolves, and poisonous snakes, he had a fair chance of survival. Food was plentiful in the river, and inland deer, wild turkeys, geese, ducks, and partridge were found in great numbers. Nut trees grew wild, as did grapes, raspberries, apples, peaches, and cherries. The soil in the back country was so rich that men talked of planting the same crops each year without fallowing, and they boasted that even seeds falling from their pockets would bear fruit.

For many, the Promised Land kept its promise, for others life in the river counties was severe and unproductive. They arrived too late in the season for crops to be planted, perhaps or winter was upon them before a satisfactory log-and-dirt hut could be built. The first farmers wrote home and advised anyone to leave for America in the winter so that they would arrive in early spring. It was also not uncommon for livestock to feed on poisonous plants and die. It took time for men—and animals—to learn the secrets of this new land and to achieve a kind of harmony with it. Most of the region's tales, however, were romances of the easy life by the river; they omitted overt suggestions of suffering, misery, privation, disease, death, and slavery in the valley. But it was all there, and it did happen.

It was through the labor of West Indian and African slaves that many Hudson Valley "aristocrats" were able to develop their large estates. Much of the land on those plantations was cleared and cared for by men in bondage. Not until 1827 did it become illegal to own or trade slaves in New York State, and some shippers were forced to turn from this lucrative business to other cargoes. But until then slaves, though sometimes quartered in the attics of their masters' homes, were usually kept in outbuildings that lacked light and ventilation. When the master suffered from extremes in temperature, the slave was lucky to survive at all in crude dwellings that afforded him only minimal protection. There were, of course, exceptions to the general treatment of slaves in the Hudson River valley. Many did only light labor around the house as menservants or worked the kitchen gardens. They assumed their masters' religions but were not allowed to sit in the same sections of the churches. Personal relations between master and slave were often close, and some were unwavering in lifelong mutual devotion. One aged slave lady, having served her master faithfully, was freed at his death, and his will provided for her full support and care by a physician. Such cases were not exceptional, nor were they the rule.

There were also examples of particularly wretched treatment of slaves in New York right up to abolition. One of the worst occurred in Manhattan in 1741, when a Negro plot "to burn down the town and kill all the white people" was allegedly uncovered.

Late Saturday night, February 28, 1741, Robert Hogg's general store on Broad Street, at the corner of Jew's Alley, in New York City, was robbed of money and goods. During the investigation that followed, Hogg's wife recalled that Christopher Wilson, a crewman on *H.M.S. Flamborough,* then stationed at the port, was a constant visitor of their boarders' servants. It was also learned that Wilson was friendly with other slaves of dubious reputation who gathered in a dive on Greenwich Street owned by John Hughson, a known "fence." Wilson told Mrs. Hogg that he had seen a Negro dividing a capful of coins with some other slaves in Hughson's place after the robbery. Two of the slaves were arrested, and Hughson and his wife

The Vanderbilt mansion, Hyde Park: east front (*John Mylod*)

The Vanderbilt main house, north portico, now a National Historic Site (*John Mylod*)

were brought before the court. The Hughsons denied everything, and were released; their house was then searched by the town constable, who found nothing. The following day, however, Mary Burton, Hughson's indentured servant, was gossiping with the constable's wife and said that Mr. Kannady "had trod over" the stolen goods. Hughson was again brought before the court and confronted with Mary's testimony; he finally admitted having received stolen property.

In the weeks that followed a series of unexplained fires destroyed the Governor's residence, a few shops, and warehouses. A woman sitting in the window of a Broadway alehouse one afternoon reported that she had overheard a group of Negroes laughing about the fires as they passed by. The following noon a chimney fire was discovered at the garrison; a week later there was another at Mrs. Hamilton's house. Captain Sarly, who lived next to Mrs. Hilton, had bought a slave from a Spanish prize ship only a few months earlier (the Negroes on board had been free seamen, but an admiralty court had condemned them to slavery anyway). After Mrs. Hilton's fire a crowd gathered in front of Sarly's house and demanded his slave. All the other slaves from the Spanish ship were also jailed. The fact that many Negroes were present at the fires and that some were even seen jumping from the burning buildings was, according to Third Justice Daniel Horsmanden, enough evidence for any man. Confessions, however, were not forthcoming even after Lieutenant-Governor George Clark offered a £100 reward for any information leading to the conviction of the incendiaries.

On April 21 profane and malleable Mary Burton was summoned to the court and, after being roughly questioned, obliged the prosecution with the testimony that it wanted to hear. She admitted under oath that she had overheard blacks in the upper rooms of Hughson's inn plotting to burn down the town. More Negroes were arrested, tried without counsel, and condemned on only the flimsiest evidence to be hanged or burned at the stake. A group of prize slaves from the West Indies, including Juan deSylva, was similarly condemned even after proof that Mary Burton could not have overheard them plotting a conspiracy as they could speak no English and she not a syllable of Spanish. Even the argument of the slaves' owners that the rigors of their first winter in the North had kept them in their quarters during the entire period when the plotting had allegedly occurred was to no avail. Mary was more explicit each time that she was called to give testimony, and her imagination was incredibly fertile.

During this Negro-plot mania, Georgia's Governor James Oglethorpe informed Clark that he had learned of a Spanish plot to "destory the magazines and considerable towns" of English North America. He added that priests had been directed to carry out these awful orders and might be disguised as teachers or dancing masters. Horsmanden, convinced that the "hand of Popery" was behind all the town's troubles and that skillful agitators, "probably Jesuits," were at work kindling public fears, sent spies in search of such emissaries.

Luckless John Ury had taken rooms in Croker's Fighting Cocks tavern about a year before the Oglethorpe letter and had settled into the business of teaching Greek and Latin. Horsmanden had Ury arrested and accused him of being a Roman Catholic priest. Miss Burton was brought before the court to swear that Ury had been a frequent visitor of Hughson's dive and had provoked much of the Negro agitation. Her imagination was beginning to provoke incredulous smiles among the townspeople and to infuriate slave owners whose chattels were being burned or hanged. It was pointed out that Mary had previously sworn that no white man other than Hughson had been involved in the conspiracies but a jailed slave who had seen that "confessions" had led to leniency for other slaves, provided the corroboration necessary to send Ury to the gallows.

A fortnight after Juan deSylva died, John Ury was hanged, after which the Negro-plot scare also seemed to die. What began in the aftermath of Hogg's robbery ended only after eleven Negroes had been burned at the stake, eighteen hanged, and fifty deported to the West Indies. John Ury and a few other white men had gone to the gallows for their alleged roles in a "popish plot," which, had it actually existed, would have made Guy Fawkes Day seem paltry in the history of conspiracies. These men all died martyrs to insane prejudice. Daniel Horsmanden, whose "conscience smote him," later confessed that he had invented much of the background information necessary to prosecute for conspiracy. But memories were short, and ignorance continued to cause the occasional execution of slaves in other parts of the Hudson valley.

Slave labor was used to propel several crude scow ferries back and forth across the river when they first entered service at various important landings. From the early days of Fort Orange, and especially after the patroonship of Rensselaerwyck had been opened for settlement in 1630, almost all traveling was done via the river. Communication between Fort Orange and Manhattan was by sloop, and homes were not built too far back from the shore. As more farmers began to clear fields inland, mill builders set up operations on creeks throughout the valley, and docks were constructed on the river nearby. Although the Dutch may have been, in Governor Thomas Dongan's words, "great improvers of the land," they nevertheless failed to develop a very good road system for travel or communications.

Prior to the English establishment of the King's Highway on both sides of the river in the eighteenth century, Dutch roads had run laterally from the Hudson and were often merely wheel ruts to sloop docks. But the King's Highway paralleled the river and generally followed paths along the valleys and watercourses which the Indians had trod for years. The subsequent clustering of homes and business inland induced boat owners throughout the valley to offer primitive ferry service. Beside the many crossings in Manhattan, enterprising river men eventually established ferry lines at Alpine, New Jersey, and Dobbs Ferry, Nyack, Verplanck's Point, Garrison, Fishkill Landing (today's Beacon), Marlborough, Milton, Poughkeepsie (across the Rondout), from the Rondout to Rhinecliff, Catskill, Hudson, Albany, Troy, and several locations above Waterford.

But in this age of the concrete cloverleaf the Hudson is no longer the highway it once was. Many old river towns share the problems of towns elsewhere that for one reason or another have been passed by and forgotten. They are only river towns now by reason of their location. Their former importance as ferry slips, sloop basins, whaling ports, or steamboat stops is recorded in local newspaper offices and recalled in articles for historical quarterlies. The sources of wealth a century ago are hinted at today in the crumbling wharves and blighted neighborhoods. The valley land and the men who belong to the land are gradually giving in to industrial growth and urban sprawl. Crop lands become parking fields and shopping centers. Orchards are sawed down for subdivisions, and new roads threaten to reshape whole business and housing districts. Many cities, from New York to Glens Falls, are caught up in projects to renew nineteenth-century neighborhoods and to reclaim valuable human resources. The reasons for change in the Hudson valley are related to the fundamental social and economic upheavals of the twentieth century. The speed of our headlong rush into the atomic future confounds the mind, and many institutions are left to memory.

"Speed! Refrigerated speed!" is the merchants' cry, and the river cannot compete. After the Erie, Champlain, and Delaware & Hudson canals were dug, the boom years in commercial transportation on the Hudson began, a process that, strangely enough, did not create a heavily industrialized river valley with coal-blackened factories spewing fly ash over the cities and their waterfronts. Heavy industry never achieved the massive proportions that the river could conceivably have supported, and it is now on the verge of disappearing. Most of the bulk shipping today leaves the valley as raw materials for other parts of the East. Steel barges full of stone, bricks, and cement go downriver from quarries above Kingston, the Rondout Creek, Clinton Point, Tomkins Cove, and Haverstraw, but they return to these landings with their gunwales high out of the water. Although the Hudson is ideal for deep-water shipping, such traffic is now being controlled to some extent by regulatory agencies and innovations in the industrial process itself. New production methods have turned many Hudson River cities into component-manufacturing and assembly centers for companies that, in turn, have deserted outmoded and inefficient waterfront locations for expanded facilities near major roadways. The river is simply no longer as important as it once was to the economies of towns like North Creek, Glens Falls, Hudson, Kingston, Poughkeepsie, Newburgh, and a dozen others scattered from its source to the sea.

After Robert Fulton's perfection of the steamboat the river became clogged with freight and passenger vessels between Albany and the Battery on the southern tip of Manhattan, but better highways, trucks, and imagination in the railroad industry have reduced the Hudson's traffic over the years to bulk cargoes of fuel oil, gasoline, petroleum by-products, bricks, trap rock, lumber, cement, processed sugar, and grain. Passenger travel on the river above New

York City is limited mainly to privately owned pleasure craft and the Day Line's daily excursion to Bear Mountain and Poughkeepsie. Sight-seeing boats still circle Manhattan, and the government-subsidized Staten Island ferry continues to offer its twenty-minute ride across New York harbor for a nickel. Passenger travel on the Hudson has decreased due to our widespread worship of the great God speed. The river has become in a sense, a neglected canal, with high-speed rail lines replacing towpaths on both banks. The Thomas E. Dewey Thruway, linking New York City and New England with Buffalo and the West, is as important today as the Hudson River-Erie Canal combination during the nineteenth century. But the pendulum will probably swing the other way in the not too distant future, as old-steamboat-like cruises to Albany become "in" trips in the social scheme of things. Then the public will once again enjoy the Hudson's scenery from a boat deck, catch glimpses of its great mansions, and recognize the sleeping figure of Rip Van Winkle in the mountain formations silhouetted against the sunset above Kingston.

The industrial complexion of the Hudson valley has altered rapidly in the last' two decades. An upsurge in the electronics industry during the 1950s transformed the tidewater region into a center for research, with International Business Machines' facilities in Kingston, Poughkeepsie, and Fishkill looming over all other competition. Although stone is still dug out of the hillsides along the river, fewer and fewer quarries continue large-scale operations. Cement companies have curtailed production in recent years, but most of the brick-baking kilns beside the Hudson have been shut down. Titanium and garnet are dug out of the ground in the upper reaches of the valley around the town of North River, but practically all the known emory deposits near Peekskill have been worked out. Elisha Otis' elevator factory in Yonkers made the skyscraper concept practical, and large sugar, lumber, copper, and bulk-fuel storage installations hug the river's edge north toward the Croton River. Paper making and the production of related by-products are dominant industries at the northern end of the industrial valley. In between, the Tri-Cities—Albany, Schenectady, and Troy—continue to develop into a dense manufacturing triangle.

The lower-tier counties below the Adirondack watershed and

Saratoga are expanding at predictable rates as business and residential complexes fan out from urban centers in ever-widening radial patterns. It is a region of predominantly small businesses scattered wherever practicality warrants the erection of one-story concrete buildings for the production of machine parts, gauges, electronic equipment, wallboard, or wearing apparel. Farms are still prevalent in the Hudson River valley, but fewer men are willing to work on them. Reliable labor for seasonal jobs like haying and fruit picking is becoming increasingly difficult to find, and wages are not generally competitive with those in industry or commensurate with the work involved. For these and a dozen similar reasons many farmers, even some with family property deeds dating back a hundred years, cannot resist the whisper of the real-estate man with an eye on his frontage. In spite of the spiritual wealth that can be derived from working the land, some river-valley farmers believe that there are just too many variables to contend with these days. Others have found that the land has become too valuable to farm when it will earn more on the home-loan investment block or is ideally situated for an industrial park. But there are also many old river farms that, even though they are not seriously operated, at least insulate their owners from the expansion around them. It is because much of the river land is not only private but also residential that heavy industry has been so well controlled along the Hudson.

There is also a whole history of river towns and industries that competition and technology have eliminated. The last vestiges of many old docks have rotted into the river or been removed. Abandoned pilings and breakwaters snag the current at low tide or stand ice-eaten in the black water. Even some tiny railheads have disappeared, swallowed up by progress and time. Buildings collapse, roof trees sag, walls cave in, and root fingers pry open the foundations, leaving in ruins all that has already been forgotten.

When waterpower was replaced by steam turbines and diesel engines, mills along the Hudson and every fair-sized creek closed down. Some became private homes, art galleries, or curiosity shops; others were simply abandoned. Gas and electricity made whale-sperm oil obsolete, and after too few years of prosperity whalers no longer sailed "around the Horn" from Hudson, Poughkeepsie, or Newburgh. In the first decade of this century a new contraption called the "refrigerator" left the Knickerbocker Ice Company without a market and forced it to vacate mammoth storage buildings all along the river which once housed tons of ice to be barged during the summer months to New York City. Sixty years later, people still refer to "iceboxes." Up in Warren County a monument in North River commemorates the "men of the drive," who logged in the upper Hudson for more than a century until the 1950s brought mechanized transportation into the lumber business.

Along with buildings and businesses that have gradually slipped into history are relics like the *Mary Powell, Queen Mary, Queen Elizabeth,* Night Line boats to Albany, the streamliner Pacemaker, and, of course, the Twentieth Century Limited. The Grand Union, United States, and other great Saratoga hotels are gone now, replaced by hamburger houses, and not many years ago the crumbling facades of the Catskill Mountain House were put to the torch one January morning by the New York State Department of Conservation. These fading symbols of a unique era of opulence and manners have been lost in the rush of a world preoccupied with making the present obsolete. We "arrive" wherever we are going as rapidly as the latest invention can take us there—but when we reach that great toll plaza at the end of the trip, where shall we have arrived? And will we have had any fun along the way?

In the last half of the nineteenth century wealthy men came to the river valley and built great homes to attest to their personal fortunes. At one time or another most of the great names in American finance have been represented in the mansion class along the Hudson. On or adjacent to properties descended from the landed Colonial class they built monuments to position and prosperity. Some of these houses were merely seasonal stopping-off places, lavishly decorated by men who were spared the income tax. Well-appointed Adirondack retreats serviced by private railroads were absurdly called "camps" by their owners while on the lower Hudson, furnishings and even whole rooms were being imported from Europe. In later years, however, more than a few of these once-flourishing estates became increasingly expensive to operate. Finally, only the government or the church could afford to maintain these extensive properties and many estates have become museums, national historic sites, or novitiate enclaves for various religious orders. Regardless of whether these estates were donated for financial or philanthropic reasons, the result is that thousands of acres have been kept out of reach of the land grabbers who would run off with a bundle at the expense of the whole river-valley community. Much of this acreage is now state or Federal park land and has been preserved for the commonweal.

The Hudson's banks from Yonkers to Troy are lined with the ornate and the insignificant. Castles dug into the mountainsides overlook the tar-paper shacks of shad fishers and river men. There is enormous incongruity along the river between the palaces of elegance and art and the run-down slum towns forever smothered in chalk dust from cement mills or soot from clay kilns. In many of these dilapidated shanty villages from New York City to North Creek, the only hope of change is in the weather. Yet in still another contrast, amid such poverty, the river's Colonial homes still stand, combining history and simple beauty; there is also a chain of eighteenth-century inns from Manhattan to Montreal. The oldest operating hotel in America, the Beekman Arms on the Post Road in Rhinebeck, still prohibits the wearing of boots in bed and limits the number of transients per bed to five.

The Marquis de Chastellux, a French nobleman who traveled as a tourist from Philadelphia to see the Saratoga battlefields a few years after they had been won, kept a journal filled with comments on his accommodations. He was impressed with the hospitality of common folk throughout the Hudson valley and praised them in his correspondence with General Washington. As Chastellux approached a household along the King's Highway, the owner would invite him and members of his party to rest in front of the fire and "have some cider." Although touched by the constant attention paid to his group, the Marquis often refused such invitations to escape the cold, knowing that the harsh December days would seem even worse when he left a warm house. The weather, however, did not discourage this Frenchman, who believed that after a long day on the trail "a good fire, a good meal, and good talk" could mellow the bitterest winter evening. For Chastellux, getting there was indeed at least half the fun.

Life's simple pleasures, which Chastellux enjoyed, were all that many people along the river ever asked for. In the nineteenth century romances bloomed as couples in rowboats rode out the rollers from the night boat to Albany. In the years between the two world wars kids skimmed shale on the river at Hyde Park every evening, waiting for those few goose-bumped seconds when the Twentieth Century would roar past at seventy miles an hour. There was plenty of activity on the railroad in those days, and if a kid saw only the red and gray boxcars of the high-speed Pacemaker freight, he knew that he had missed the Pacemaker itself by ten minutes. Freight trains are too infrequent for kids these days, but they're much longer, and counting cars is more challenging. Because the Penn Central Railroad follows the Hudson all the way to Albany it is sometimes difficult to find a place where one can legally walk down to the river's edge except to the north of the capital or in the high country of the Adirondacks. Breakfast at daybreak on an Adirondack mountain trail cannot be described but must be experienced and enjoyed. At the other end of the valley, when the glass palisades of Manhattan turn crimson, sun worshipers gather on park benches above Riverside Drive to watch their idol drop behind the New Jersey hills. It is their time of day, and for a while at least they are oblivious of the rush around them. The shadows in the Catskills at dusk also bring to life the smoky landscapes of Thomas Cole, Frederick Church, Asher Durand, and other artists of the Hudson River School and there is a new valley seen.

But the Hudson's moods must be experienced to be truly understood and appreciated. They change constantly. New aspects, unseen, unknown before, appear each day, during the day, and with the coming of another season. As we meander toward tidewater, contrasts and continuity in the river valley are immediate and obvious. The Hudson is really two rivers with two distinct characters—and magnificent beauty as their common cohesive.

TWO

AT THE HUDSON's mouth, New York City completely dwarfs all the other river cities and ports, yet the river's source is still locked in mountain wilderness. There is no great city there. Paving machines have come to within only eight or ten miles of Mt. Marcy's summit, and the scarcity of improved roads make this central Adirondack region relatively inaccessible.

On the slopes of Tahawas, "cloud splitter" to the Indians, at a point 1,000 feet below the peak of mile-high Mt. Marcy, is Lake Tear of the Clouds, the beginning of one of the shortest and greatest runs to the sea. Lake Tear is part of a capillary network of creeks, small rivers, and streams that irrigate the Adirondack watershed and whose rushing waters combine to keep the Hudson running swiftly downhill to Troy. The nature of this upper river is almost totally different from that of the tidewater Hudson. It is a quick-coursing spillway full of bread-loaf boulders and beaver dams, not unlike hundreds of other mountain streams that follow the deep ravines created when the Adirondacks thrust their craggy land masses into the sky and were landscaped by the last glacial icecap. Although some of the glacial debris in this geological storehouse dates from about 25 million years ago, the general terrain is quite young. The myriad natural amphitheaters and lakes splattered through these mountains were dug out, reshaped, or filled less than 10,000 years ago.

High in the mountains near Summit Water, Lake Tear's older and less popular name, there is the luxury of almost total silence. The mountain floor is deep-piled with leaves and pine needles, which silence footfalls and cushion noise. Hemlock, balsam, spruce, cedar, birch, ash, pine, and poplar reach for the sun and come closer to touching it here than in any other part of New York State. In winter it seems as if only a few birds and the cracking of bark splitting sound in the woods. Buried in hip-high snow, shallow pools bubble out of frosted dams. But the dominant sense of calm is not seriously challenged. This serenity in a neon world is precious indeed, and we can forget, contemplate, rethink, and renew. When Henry Thoreau wrote "in wilderness is the preservation of the world" he could not have characterized this uncluttered patch of the galaxy more accurately.

Out of earshot of its source, Lake Tear, the Opalescent River, plunging down from the Feldspar Brook, divides the sprawling black piles and storage silos of the National Lead Company's titanium mine and mill. This complex is the first big industry on the river and the last for many miles. Near the town of Newcomb the combined waters of numerous lakes and streams bend south and become large enough to be called the Hudson. The river then curves south-southeast and runs white over rocks at North Creek.

It is there that a Delaware & Hudson train waited to take Theodore Roosevelt to Albany, where he changed trains and raced for Buffalo to assume the Presidency after William McKinley's assassination. Roosevelt was camped on Mt. Marcy when a woodsman brought the news at midnight that President McKinley had been shot. The Vice-President was advised to wait for sunup before proceeding to the D & H depot at North Creek. Roosevelt, however, informed his guides that it was their prerogative to remain in camp until daybreak but that he was preparing to leave immediately with or without them. Not far from a ranger's cabin on Route 28N there is a tablet that reads:

Near This Point
While Driving Hastily from Tahawus Club
to North Creek at 2:15 AM Sept 14 1901
Theodore Roosevelt Became President of
the United States as William McKinley
Expired in Buffalo—
Relay Drivers

David Hunter   Tahawus Club to Tahawus
Orrin Kellogg   Tahawus to Aiden Lair
Michael Cronin   Aiden Lair to North Creek

When Roosevelt stopped to change horses at Aiden Lair Lodge, proprietor Mike Cronin decided to drive the team the rest of the way to North Creek. Sometime after the old Bull Moose was in the White House, there was a story that Cronin had sold the shoes that his horses had worn on that rugged night ride. In fact, he was said to have sold several barrels of the authentic shoes. Years later, however, Cronin's daughter confessed in an interview that not a single horseshoe had ever been sold. Mike Cronin simply added a little more each year to the story he liked to tell.

Route 28N has been paved since Roosevelt followed it to North Creek, but much of the country around it is still unchanged. Summer camps and small farms claim a portion of the land, but in some spots once-cleared pastures are reverting to their original wild state. This whole area is part of the Adirondack Forest Preserve, a park encompassing more than 5 million acres, the largest in the nation. Almost half of this land is state-owned and practically all the state land is wilderness; it will remain "forever wild" as prescribed by an amendment to the New York State Constitution. The rest of the land within the irregular "blue line" on the map is private property consisting of hotels, summer camps, hunting lodges, farms, mines, commercial lumber enterprises, and untouched forests. The noted Adirondack woodsman John Cheney once said of the Marcy region, "there are woods there that would take a lifetime to hunt over." Manhattan is a monument to man's work, but along the Adirondack Hudson there are thousands and thousands of acres that man has left free. Anyone who takes the glass towers of Manhattan for granted is incredibly foolish, but if he also ignores the Hudson and its wilderness preserve, there is no limit to his deprivation. Millions of people swarm in New York City, but the population of Essex County does not equal the number of deer in its confines. The traveling time between these two ends of the river valley, however, is less than one working day. Only zero imagination or the confining influence of poverty keep these poles apart.

Towns and cities are included within the "blue line" on the map, but the larger ones are in the southeastern portion of the park. Newcomb, Minerva, Riparius, Johnsburg, The Glen, and other such villages consist of a handful of houses each, a few stores that provide everything from mail service to millinery, an intersection, and one or two churchyard cemeteries. Many of the headstones in these small plots are old and have become more than simple grave markers with terse inscriptions. More than a few of these stones are chipped and rain-washed, looking like salt licks in the grass, but beneath them rest men and women who came to these mountains in the eighteenth century and battled the wilderness. It is possible to stand inside the fallen iron fences of such burial grounds and to see an Adirondack landscape that has changed very little in the last 200 years. At such a moment, time past and future coalesce in the present and are linked by human awareness of the challenge in this land.

The countryside near Minerva, especially around Mink Pond, was a favorite summering spot for Winslow Homer. He came here often in the 1890s, ostensibly to fish, but he always went away with sketches and unfinished studies that would be completed in his studio at Prout's Neck, Maine. This "Adirondack Period" in Homer's work not only reveals the mastery of his watercolor technique but also brings alive the special nature of these magnificent mountains and the unique brand of men who roamed them. He conveyed the rugged, sometimes hostile, feeling of mountain streams and the upper Hudson or turned his washes to the quiet beauty of a lone fisherman on a glassy lake. Winslow Homer knew well the guides and mountain men and captured their beguiling spirit. He understood them and painted from this inner knowledge. His "Adirondack Guide" could have been John Cheney or Mitchell Sabattis, mountaineers who almost merged into nature's fabric. Homer's skill does not call attention to itself but is devoted instead to revealing the "stuff" of the things he saw.

John Cheney's skill as a woodsman was legendary. Born to the woods and at home with the elements, Cheney, like other Adirondack guides, was an unpretentious man who preferred understatement to rhetoric and was more impressed by bringing down a wily catamount than by sharing bedrolls with famous people. And he had done both.

On one camping trip he guided a pair of men through the notch at Indian Pass in a day-long downpour, weather that scoffers would call typical in the Adirondacks. One fellow had a bad cold and a wicked pack to cart, but with only one or two daylight hours remaining Cheney had to rush to make camp and had no time even to brew some fresh shackleberry tea to ease the man's sore throat. Both campers were enthusiastic about their "excursion" into the woods despite the weather, but their experience and assistance to Cheney were minimal at best.

He set about making camp by felling a dead tree and splitting it to the heart in order to get enough dry chips for kindling. He kept the chips dry with his coat until the pile caught fire and grew large enough to take wet wood. Then to provide meager shelter for the night he thatched the frame of an abandoned wigwam with boughs of balsam fir. For a supply of fire wood, he measured three or four trees by eye and dropped them with such accuracy that they fell next to the fire without crashing through the wigwam. For flooring blankets from the packs were covered with leaves and branches; they would have made a fine flooring if everything had not been so water-logged. Cheney then cooked bacon on coals by the fire.

Despite the bone-chilling rain that was still coming down "like all nature," the men found that after supper their lean-to, which was nothing more than a leaky shed open toward the fire, had begun to take on a homey aspect. The man's sore throat was better, and he told tales of sailing "around the Horn" on a trip from California. Each man related stories of his own world, and Cheney had almost finished his second pipe when a wind came up, began blowing smoke into the shed, and forced everybody out. Cheney countered with a wall of saplings and brush, which seemed to suffice until more gusts

"The Pioneer" by Winslow Homer (1836–1910) (*The Metropolitan Museum of Art. Purchase, 1910. Amelia B. Lazarus Fund.*)

"Camp Fire" by Winslow Homer (*The Metropolitan Museum of Art. Gift of Henry Keney Pomeroy, 1927.*)

blew the fire into the barrier, burning it and nearly destroying the wigwam. Then the rain changed to snow, which blew into all corners of the hut. With smoke filling the hut in great puffs Cheney advised the men to keep their mouths close to the ground for air and, before dropping off from exhaustion, remarked that, as long as it had "taken to blow," it was a comfort that he had cut down most of the trees "that would be likely to fall down and crush us during the night."

The storm, however, did not ruin the camping trip, which ended a few days later after the men had climbed Marcy and Cheney had escorted his two employers to North Creek, where he left them on the road back to civilization.

The Cedar, Indian, and Boreas rivers empty into the Hudson before it turns to parallel Route 28 at the town of North River. Farther south the Schroon River, which flows from Schroon Lake, snakes into the Hudson west of Warrensburg. From there to Hadley the Hudson becomes a river, plunging rapidly through narrow cuts and widening out at lazy bends.

In 1930 the Sacandaga River, which flows into the Hudson from the west, was harnessed by a dam at Conklingville to create the Sacandaga Reservoir, a water reserve as large as Lake George. Today it provides water for hydroelectric power and controlled release into the Hudson during periods of drought. Its outlet is one of the Hudson's largest tributaries, and the two join at Hadley. The Hudson bends east at Corinth and flows toward the hydroelectric plant nine miles from Glens Falls. This whole region is lumber country and in the boom years of the great drives the river was alive with logs being floated downstream to the pulp mills at Glens Falls, the Hudson's first large manufacturing town. Those lumber drives in a way resembled western cattle roundups. Logs came boiling down the river in bunches, to be sorted out in holding ponds, according to company brands. The men who kept the drive moving were as tough a group of "cowboys" as you would ever want to meet. And staying upright on a spinning balsam trunk was every bit as difficult as riding the "hurricane deck" of a horse that doesn't want you there. But pulpwood is now trucked to the mills at Glens Falls and piled haphazardly in high mounds. Lumbering is a matter-of-fact business, and the traditions of the drive have been replaced by a more efficient routine. The pulpwood industry is big in the northern counties, which are key suppliers of paper to New York City's giant publishing industry. Glens Falls and South Glens Falls also manufacture wood by-products in addition to wallpaper and paper napkins, plates, bags, cartons, and wrapping material.

The Indians called Glens Falls Chepuntuc, or "Hard Place to Get Around," because of the rocks and white water. A man from Dutchess County named Wing owned these falls, which bore his name for a time, but he sold the rights to John Glen for the price of a meal. As soon as the deal and the meal were finished, it is said, Glen posted road signs reporting the new name all the way to Albany. The falls are perhaps best known for a small cave in the rocks, in which Hawk-eye, Uncas, and their companions hid from Iroquois savages in James Fenimore Cooper's *The Last of the Mohicans*. Today the rumble of traffic on a bridge over the falls drowns the romance of Cooper's legend, and milk-colored bilge wooshes into the river from a hole in a mill wall.

At Hudson Falls the river makes a right-angle turn, ending 100 miles of sea-level–seeking twists and bends. There a V-shaped dam harnesses the river's flow for a power supply, and old stone bridge piers stand forlornly in the middle of the stream with nothing to hold. From there to the Ambrose Light the river, widening out through pastures and wood lots, runs south with very little rushing for about 200 miles.

At Fort Edward there is no fort today, only a rock marker where the old stockade once stood and signs at the outer defenses. But Fort Edward was once an important jumping-off point for the portage to Lake Champlain and a vital defensive link during the French and Indian War. The Champlain canal bends northeast there, and the Delaware & Hudson tracks parallel its locks as far as Whitehall. John Burgoyne, the playboy playwright of the English general staff, marched on General Philip Schuyler at Fort Edward during the Revolution only to find the stockade evacuated and Schuyler's trail blocked by felled trees and ruined bridges.

It was near Fort Edward too that the tragedy of Jane McCrea was enacted in 1777. Jane, a preacher's daughter, was engaged to Lieutenant David Jones, a loyalist militiaman camped with Burgoyne's forces. One muggy afternoon an Indian came into camp carrying in his belt a scalp with long, lustrous hair. An English prisoner recognized it as that of her neighbor Jane McCrea. Burgoyne had offered a bounty for scalps but had forbidden his Indians to take them from anyone not in arms. A Hessian officer wrote, however, that Indians often went on the prowl in small groups as bounty hunters.

"Poor Jenny McCrea" had planned to see her fiancé near Fort Edward and had refused to escape downriver with her brother as the English advanced. She preferred to remain at the home of a Tory friend. The following day a Negro boy ran to the rebel garrison to report that the two women had been captured by a group of Indians and were being taken toward their camp. Men detached to rescue the women engaged the savages not far from the Tory widow's home. In the brief skirmish that followed, Jane McCrea was unfortunately shot and killed by accident. The Indians escaped unharmed and returned to the English lines but not before removing Jane's scalp.

In another version of the McCrea tragedy Jane's fiancé had sent two Indians ahead to escort her back to camp and had promised to reward them for her safe passage. While on the trail she was met instead by members of a scouting party who treated her with civility until an argument arose among them over to whom the prisoner actually belonged. In the middle of this "discussion" one of the Indians buried his tomahawk in the young woman's skull, scalped her, and returned to camp for the reward. Burgoyne was furious with the Indians and restricted their movements so tightly after the McCrea incident that many deserted his force for good. Lieutenant Jones petitioned the General to be relieved of his military obligations and, when he was refused, deserted to Canada.

The American General Horatio Gates realized the enormous propaganda value in Jane's death and castigated Burgoyne and the English for hiring savages to "scalp Europeans and the descendants of Europeans." In a published letter he condemned Burgoyne for behaving cruelly and ungentlemanly in the sad case in which a preacher's daughter was "dressed to meet her promised husband but met her murderers." This accusation was not true, but it helped to enrage Americans and brought many previously uncommitted colonists

This argument over Jane McCrea ended with her death. (*Glens Falls Insurance Company, Glens Falls, New York*)

into the field against Burgoyne. Many of those who had been un-willing to oppose King George III now irrevocably cast their lot with the rebels.

U.S. Route 4 follows the old roads over which the British and Americans fought in the battles of the Hudson. The forests that hampered Burgoyne's caravan march on General Gates and his American forces ten miles south of Schuylerville at Bemis Heights have been cleared since that conflict, in order to provide grazing land for dairy herds. Pastures and crop land run to the river, and many forgotten battlefields hump their backs to the scratches of the plow and are reclaimed. There is a panorama of gently rolling landscapes blotched with wizened locust trees and stands of maples that survived the battles and are still alive.

Bergamot, orange hawkweed, and some unnamed wild flowers crowd the hill around the Saratoga Battle Monument in the Schuylerville cemetery. The original town of Saratoga has been called Schuylerville since 1777, and patriots from all American wars are buried in the ground around the monument. In a mural relief on one of the monument's ground-floor walls a bronze Indian scalps Jane McCrea. In another scene on another wall Mrs. Philip Schuyler set fire to a wheat field to prevent Burgoyne from making use of its crop. From the top of this granite-and-steel tower the entire country-side appears blanketed in soft green velvet with a channel cut where the Hudson flows. The view north toward Burgoyne's route is un-obstructed; in the distance the smoke geyser from a Glens Falls cement plant seems motionless. To the east the Green Mountains rise up out of Vermont. A mile from the Battle Monument, down the steep hill past the restored Schuyler mansion, the river runs under overhanging willow trees and is about wide enough for a "Washington toss."

General Burgoyne was finally defeated at Bemis Heights, and it was near old Saratoga that the defeated British soldiers were ferried across the Hudson to begin their march for Boston and eventual de-portation. According to the Saratoga Treaty those soldiers who had outlived the battle were also out of the war for good. Most of the prisoners were moved from one camp to another, however, for fear the English might renege and bring them back into another theater of the war. The battle of Saratoga wrecked British hopes of controlling the Hudson and was a clear enough indication to the French that the time had come to join the American rebels in bringing the English King to his knees.

One of the most unique monuments to any man is the marble leg at Saratoga National Historic Park, Bemis Heights, that commemorates Benedict Arnold's heroism at Saratoga and Quebec. At Saratoga a british musket blast struck Arnold in the leg during the hectic fighting around Freeman's farm, but the leg was not amputated as is sometimes supposed. The booted leg, commissioned by John Watts DePeyster of Tivoli, New York, and carved by George Bissell of Poughkeepsie, is a romantic symbol of Arnold's courage before his treasonous league with the English Major John André. Arnold, however, is remembered for his honor and courage only at Saratoga.

West of the old battlefield is Saratoga Springs, the center of New York's spa country. There in August the nation's best thoroughbreds run the mile at one of the most elegant racetracks in the country. In August too the Saratoga Performing Arts Center, the summer home of the Philadelphia Orchestra, caters to the culturally minded, who also occasionally turn out to be members of the racing establishment. The springs that once attracted thousands have lost some of their appeal, but for the last century people have been flocking from all over to see and be seen at the races. Horses are auctioned in a modern concrete arena that appears to have been built to compete with the Arts Center, for it looks more like a small concert hall than a market for horses. People still come to Saratoga to bet and buy horseflesh, but the old black-tie yearling sales have yielded to relatively mundane affairs with more than a sprinkling of business suits. The last vestiges of the era when the big hotels at Saratoga Springs were filled and "the season" crowded with enough glamorous parties to last a lifetime have all but disappeared. Now billboards along the roads to Saratoga Springs and the racetrack quicken a bettor's pulse with the reminder that "General Gates Won at Saratoga; You Can Too."

Between Schuylerville and Troy the Hudson is fed from the east by the Hoosic River and from the west by its largest tributary, the Mohawk. The latter cascades into the Hudson over the Cohoes falls

The deserted Erie Canal at Waterford

and, with the Erie division of the New York State Barge Canal, connects the western reaches of the state to tidewater shipping. The traffic through the locks has been drastically reduced over the last fifty years by the greater importance of rail and over the road truck transportation. The Champlain division of the barge canal is also in operation, and fuel barges can be lifted above the Waterford rapids where Hudson's crewmen took the shallow soundings that ended his up-river voyage. Commercial canal boats are built specially for these locks, with only inches to spare on each side; some of the walls and bows show the scars of miscalculation. Usually, however, commercial barges pass through without incident, the deckhands holding heavy rope mats between bows and lock walls for protection. Pushed by tugs like the *Cardinal* and *Mobil 9,* a barge eases into the lock, and the water forced back along its sides acts as a natural cushion. The barge is raised rapidly by powerful pumps, and in less than fifteen minutes the whole operation is completed.

Summer brings pleasure boatmen through the Champlain Canal in increasing numbers each year, and a regular schedule is maintained fairly closely to cope with the heavier traffic. One lock operator said that many of the July and August seamen are unacquainted with the standard navigational marking devices: "Half of them rent boats for a month and don't even know what a buoy is. It takes them a hundred and fifty miles from New York to Waterford to find out that a red light on a buoy doesn't mean that you have to stop. Believe me, I don't even know how they make it to the locks at Troy."

Troy, just south of Waterford, was at one time the detachable shirt-collar capital of the East. The shirts from Troy factories these days, however, have collars sewn on, with little buttons at the tips to keep them from curling up. Church and ship bells were also cast there once, but pig iron, baked goods, shirts, and scientific instruments are Troy's major products today. Across the river, in Watervliet, an old cannon arsenal contrasts sharply with the remains of a Shaker village founded by Ann Lee after she came to the Hudson valley from England to escape religious persecution. "Mother Lee," accompanied by cautious farmers who were also true "believers," established her colony in 1775. The residents eventually expanded their industry and prospered, selling brooms, spinning wheels, and baskets throughout the Hudson River valley and New England. Mother Lee did not hold with the fighting in the Revolution and often said so. There was at least one instance when, after speaking out against rebel action, she was jailed for her own protection. Her little colony has since been swallowed up in Albany's urbanizing expansion.

Highways fan out from the glossy new capital complex, cross bridges, and form a web connecting satellite towns to the central city. Once known as Beverwyck and Fort Orange, Albany continues to undergo transformation and feel the pains of redevelopment, as do most of the other towns in the Tri-City area, which now has a total population of well over 1 million. Albany, however, has come full circle in rail transportation.

During the nineteenth century, when Hudson River Railroad trains ended their runs in East Albany, westbound passengers were ferried across the river and taken by carriage to the New York Central's Albany terminal. The Hudson River and New York Central were separate railroads in those years and were not merged into one system until Commodore Cornelius Vanderbilt finally gained control of Central stock. After that the railroad from Manhattan to Buffalo became the New York Central, and Albany emerged as a major division point. The Boston & Albany and Delaware & Hudson connected with the New York Central there, and less than a generation ago 100 passenger trains cleared the Albany yards daily. Trains like the Montreal Limited, the Wolverine, the New York Special, and the Southwestern Limited stopped in Albany to change steam locomotives, uncouple Pullmans for Montreal via the D & H, and to take on mail and new crews. A new station was opened in Albany in 1900, and one reporter wrote that "it was an inspiration to study the architecture and the chandeliers with their incandescent lights." Two years later the Central inaugurated one of the world's greatest luxury trains, the Twentieth Century Limited.

Traveling west as train No. 25 and eastbound as No. 26, the Century was the railroad's pride for more than fifty years and made the run from New York to Chicago in sixteen hours. It cruised at 75 miles an hour and took precedence over everything on the railroad.

In its great days the Century was an all-Pullman flyer with deluxe drawing rooms, staterooms, single and double bedrooms, showers, valets, barbers, maid service, secretaries, manicurists, gourmet meals, fresh flowers on every table, impeccably mannered stewards, and a partial refund for every hour that it was late. The dining car catered to every taste and had a reputation of being one of the best restaurants in the country. On one occasion, a frequent commuter to Chicago wished to order lobster Newburg on toasted corn bread, but it was not on the menu. The steward noted that there was cold lobster on the menu, which at least gave the chef something to begin with. The gentleman had a drink and was reassured a few minutes later that everything would be ready soon. Two more cocktails later the steward finally appeared with the lobster Newburg and apologized for the delay. It seems that the chef had been forced to make a pan of fresh corn bread and cook it before filling the order.

In 1912 five cars of the eastbound Century jumped the tracks two miles south of Hyde Park and plunged into the Hudson. Miraculously the thick river ice supported the steel cars and passengers climbed from the windows of the Pullmans "Mancelona" and "The Phelps." Pieces of track were thrown 100 yards out onto the ice, and the trucks were torn from the undercarriages of the sleepers, but incredibly enough no one was killed in the wreck.

From the late 1940s on, this high-speed express carried three diesels and from fifteen to eighteen cars with gleaming stainless-steel trim. It stopped in few stations, and railroad men remembered the year, month, day, and hour that it was flagged down in their towns. After large conventions in New York and Notre Dame-Army games at Yankee Stadium, section after section of the Century would leave Grand Central ten minutes apart, carrying politicians and Irish fans back to Chicago. But traditional service began to disintegrate on the Century, and by the mid-1960s no one wanted to spend sixteen hours going to Chicago by train when he could fly there in less than two. The New York Central saw things the same way and did nothing to improve service or encourage passenger travel.

The Twentieth Century's sixty-five-year history ended unceremoniously on December 2, 1967, when its red carpet was rolled out for the last time. At Croton-Harmon a dozen men, a woman, and a boy stood on the platform to watch train no. 25 pull out. Its poorly tuned diesels coughed sparks and the fireman's hand was heavy on the horn all the way out of the station, but few waited on the platform to see the blue-lit lettering of the Twentieth Century disappear around a bend in the roadbed. The New York Central has since merged with the Pennsylvania; a year after the Century was phased out, the Penn Central closed its Albany station. Today, with long-haul passenger service slashed to the bone, a new station with window walls and plastic seats has been built across the river in Rensselaer. Most of the Central's freight is handled below Albany, at Selkirk.

Not far up the hill from the river, in the midst of Albany's business crush, is General Philip Schulyer's mansion, "The Pastures," now maintained by the state as a historic monument. Schuyler's home was once a stopping-off place for all men of position and fame who had business in Albany. General Burgoyne sat at table with Schuyler here after being defeated at Saratoga and later praised the General's gracious hospitality before the House of Commons. Burgoyne was doubly impressed with his treatment at the Pastures because it was he who had ordered Schuyler's Schuylerville house burned to the ground.

On Christmas Day 1780, General Schuyler paid Chastellux the honor of allowing him to read personal war correspondence from General Washington concerning military affairs in the Northern Department during the crucial period of the Saratoga campaign. It was in 1780 also that Schuyler's daughter Elizabeth was married to young Alexander Hamilton, who later established a forerunner of the New York *Post*. The wedding was undoubtedly the most gala affair held in the Schuyler mansion, and until Hamilton's untimely death in a duel with Aaron Burr in 1804 the couple often returned to the Pastures.

Even as a seventeenth-century Dutch trading settlement the Beverwyck region was an important commercial center, almost from its beginning. Its lines of communication crisscrossed the Hudson-Mohawk basin, connecting New England and the north country with the most important means of transportation and news: the Hudson. Turnpikes began and ended at the river, and ferry owners at Albany were prosperous. In the winter river traffic shifted from sailing vessels to sleighs, and farmers brought produce and hay over the frozen Hudson from Rensselaerwyck's large farming estates and island farms below today's capital area.

The Shodack Islands separate the Hudson south of Albany, and it is among these long, slender, finger-like land masses that Mr. Littlepage, in Cooper's *Satanstoe*, narrowly escaped death with his sleighing party during the March breaking-up of the ice. At Coeymans bricks dry in the sun on the lip of the river, and at the turn of the century paper was milled there.

In 1958 Captain Leroy Coon piloted the Grace Line's *Santa Paula* up "the ditch," a 300-foot-wide channel north of Kingston, and achieved the distinction of docking the largest passenger vessel ever to call at Albany. Cutting his speed first to half and then to dead slow, Coon guided the 584-foot ocean liner through the shallows near Coxsackie, and held his breath off New Baltimore, where only six inches of water separated the ship's keel from the rock below. This publicity cruise ended happily enough with a reception in Albany and the *Santa Paula* returned to New York City the following day for its official harbor welcome.

Under continual harassment by the English during the Revolution, a whole New England whaling community was forced to seek safer waters, and its members chose an upriver port in New York. Practically the entire population moved to Claverack Landing, subsequently changing its name to Hudson. After the war the whaling business again improved, and in 1797 Captain Solomon Bunker's *American Hero*, appropriately enough, tied up at the Hudson docks with the largest single cargo of sperm oil that the United States had seen up until that time. (There was no vegetation on the flats between Hudson and Athens in the early days, and it is believed by some historians that Henry Hudson's *Half Moon* may have run aground there.) Seal fishing was also an important industry in Hudson until about 1800, when the tanning of skins from the Falkland Islands was curtailed. Most of the leather was made into shoes and exported, along with candles, beef, pork, and barrel staves. Hudson was a thriving village and today is one of the most architecturally interesting cities in the river valley. On streets a hundred miles from the ocean you can catch a glimpse of a coastal seaport, but this image eventually fades and disappears against a backdrop of Catskill Mountains and the A & P.

For more than four centuries men have come to the region above

Catskill across the river from Hudson to dig rock from the ground and fashion it for practical use. Algonquian Indians from all over the East came to dig flint out of a quarry near Coxsackie. Up the road from where flint axes, weapons, and tools have been found gun powder and high explosives are manufactured now. Indian industry was limited, but contemporary engineers mass-produce cement from the rock for use in the new quarries of Manhattan.

The whole region west of the city of Catskill was once important for its rich deposits of limestone and bluestone, and it was there that characters from German folk tales were Americanized by the Hudson valley's most famous storyteller, Washington Irving. As the Catskill Creek flows into the Hudson, it bisects the city of Catskill. Some local wizards still speak of the thunder that rumbles in the mountains behind the city as being merely the ghosts of Hudson's crew playing tenpins. It is in these same mountains that Irving's Rip Van Winkle sat down with his dog and napped. A few Greene County "historians" believe that they know where Mrs. Van Winkle was standing when she burst a blood vessel and died while arguing with a peddler, but this is only conjecture.

One of the most significant landmarks along the Hudson River's Middle Grounds above Kingston was the Catskill Mountain House, which, for more than a century, perched on a rock outcropping high behind Van Winkle's town. A boarder at this resort could look east as far as the Taconic Mountains or in the evening see a steamboat salute as it passed by far below. He dined with world-famous citizens or was one himself. He rode up the hill to the Mountain House on one of Otis' cog railways and in later years saw the ferry at Catskill replaced by the two-lane Rip Van Winkle Bridge. The Hudson River School painters recorded and rerecorded the view from the Mountain House but admitted that it was impossible to get onto canvas what they saw. Cooper's Natty Bumppo summed up the panorama here as "all creation."

From its modest beginning as an unpretentious cottage in 1823, the Mountain House developed into a massive monument to the Neoclassic style in architecture. Other hotels made inroads into the tourist business around Catskill, but none ever attained the stature or captured the charm of the Mountain House. Cooper; Irving; William Cullen Bryant; Henry James; Presidents Grant, Arthur, and

Theodore Roosevelt; General Sherman; Alexander Graham Bell; and Oscar Wilde were only a few of the famous people who came there to refresh themselves with the eye-goggling view above the Hudson.

The first twenty years of this century were good for the Mountain House, but social change began to undermine the notions of gentility implicit in this kind of retreat. A signal change was the addition of an automobile garage. From then on the place was never quite the same. After World War II this great white whale of a building was sold, resold, and finally abandoned. Ghostlike and ghastly, exposed to the weather, and vulnerable to senseless vandalism, the Mountain House slowly died. Scavengers came to pick over and rip out what they wanted. Staircases down which countless beautiful women had paraded with their escorts were splintered or torn away from the walls. The walls of salons in which Civil War generals had reminisced about strategy were pockmarked by thrown bricks or defaced by obscene graffiti. A finishing blow came in the early 1960s when a hurricane severely damaged the roof and porches. This battered, half-collapsed building was finally burned to the ground by the state conservation department, which now owns the land. In the gloom of an early winter morning, area residents on their way to work in Catskill could see smoke curling up from the hill to the west and they knew that the Mountain House was now history.

The Esopus Creek flows south from Ashokan, turns abruptly behind Kingston, and swings north to join the Hudson at Saugerties. Saugerties' tidy little harbor, cupped in the hillside, is ideal for the shallow-draught runabouts that skim like water bugs across the Hudson's eel grass in Esopus Meadows south of Kingston. A lighthouse helped to keep ships off the mud flats there for more than a century, but like similar "lights" at Tarrytown and Hudson it has been replaced recently by an automatic buoy. Such warning devices blink at timed intervals, ring a bell, or blow a horn and can be activated by a blast from a ship's whistle. During the spring and summer Coast Guard buoy tenders replace markers dragged away by ice floes in winter, in order to ensure their precise positioning for tidewater navigation.

Kingston crowds a hill over the Rondout Creek and was an important landing long before the English gave the town its present name. In the eighteenth century canal boats by the thousands waited at the mouth of the Rondout for tugs to tow them south and the famous steamboat *Mary Powell* made Kingston her upriver terminal. The state capital was established there during the Revolution after unsafe conditions had driven it from New York, White Plains, Yonkers, Fishkill, and Poughkeepsie. Today Kingston is replacing nineteenth-century buildings with modern structures, but it is not unmindful of its traditions and preserves its historic houses.

The Kingston-Rhinecliff toll bridge is anchored to the east bank of the Hudson near Barrytown. From there to Poughkeepsie there are many private estates that date from the middle and late eighteenth century. Homes belonging to Livingstons, Vanderbilts, Mills, Roosevelts, Delanos, Astors, portrait painter and inventor Samuel F. B. Morse, and others were once prominent in this central region of the river valley, but most have been converted for institutional housing. Religious orders have also acquired land and constructed new buildings on bluffs overlooking the Hudson. In the early years of the nineteenth century, on land bought from the Jesuits, who knew it had no water, Mother Cabrini told drillers where to dig, and the resulting well has been serving her home and school ever since. "Holy husband" Father Divine owned a large tract just south of Mother Cabrini's, near Crum Elbow; east of this bend in the river is St. Andrews on-the-Hudson, a large Jesuit novitiate, where priest and palaeontologist Pierre Teilhard de Chardin is buried in a simple grave. The river is deep at the crook in Crum Elbow, and ships sometimes took on water from the springs there for sale in the West Indies.

From the Catskills down to the Highlands below Newburgh, the Hudson's west shore is a great fruit belt. Apples are the dominant crop, but pears, berries, and grapes are also grown for profit on the uneven terrain of the Shawangunk Mountain chain. On the stepped sides of Illinois Mountain across from Poughkeepsie growers pack their climate-controlled cold-storage warehouses with millions of boxes of apples annually. Together with a few cold-storage plants in northern Dutchess and Columbia counties, the combined output of this apple region is the largest in the state. Rhine wine seems to suggest a certain contradiction in the Hudson valley, but it too is produced along with all the other variations on the grape that the sun brings to fruition on the hillsides near Highland, New York.

Highland is also the western terminus of the Poughkeepsie Railroad and Mid-Hudson Bridges. The cantilevered steelwork of the railroad bridge, which was opened in 1888, carries Penn Central freight trains east and west; it was the first span to be built across the river below Albany. Many crews rowing in the four-mile Intercollegiate Regatta prepared to sprint near the stone foundations of the railroad bridge, and a quarter-mile south, First Ward boys from Poughkeepsie dove for coins thrown from the decks of Day liners.

Uppuquiipising (pronounced "oh-pooki-ipis-ing") was an Indian word, meaning "the reed-covered lodge by the little watering place," from which the name Poughkeepsie is derived. Common usage finally settled on its present spelling from about two dozen variations. The stream that the Indians meant flows into the river about a mile south of the city, and not far from there the Matthew Vassar house still stands. About two miles east of his estate Vassar built a monument to himself in the form of a women's college.

The Mid-Hudson Bridge, like the Kingston-Rhinecliff Bridge, replaced a long-operating ferry line and increased the inactivity of the waterfront. It is absurd that a city the size of Poughkeepsie has no facilities for deep-draught vessels, but because of poor city-management there are none there or in almost all the other upriver cities.

One of the oldest ferry lines on the Hudson was replaced in 1963 by the two-lane Beacon-Newburgh bridge, which carries Interstate Route 84 across the river. Chartered by King George II in 1743, this ferry line ran from Newburgh to Fishkill Landing and was especially important during the Revolution after Washington moved his army to Temple Hill near New Windsor and had established headquarters at Newburgh. East from the Hudson at Fishkill, a valley formed by the Pawling Mountains creates the beginnings of a natural roadway to New England. Enoch Crosby, a double agent for the Americans during the Revolution, was held "captive" in Fishkill's Dutch church to protect his true identity, which few men knew, before he was allowed to "escape"; the character Harvey Birch in Cooper's drama *The Spy* is based on Crosby. The old black-walnut tree across from what was called the "Wharton house" in this novel was a whipping post during the Revolution, after which it was made into a pulpit for the Dutch church and is still used in religious services.

At Cornwall the water's of Newburgh bay are funneled into a deep-channel cut through the Highlands. The most ancient rocks in the lower Hudson valley are the exposed Pre-Cambrian granites of Storm King, Bull Hill, Crow's Nest, Breakneck, and Dunderberg Mountains. Because of mud at the northern gateway to the Highlands New York City's fresh-water aqueduct from upstate reservoirs had to be sunk several hundred feet before it could be anchored safely in the Hudson's bedrock.

Pollepel, Poleppers, Pelopars, or Palopel Island is just north of Breakneck Mountain at the upper gateway to the Highlands. The deed books in the Dutchess County Clerk's office record it as a piece of land bounded on the north by the Hudson River, on the east by the Hudson River, on the south by the Hudson River, and on the west by the Hudson River. Today the island, with collapsing remains of an arsenal, built by Francis Bannerman to house his second-hand military supplies, has become state park land. Boatmen once made a regular practice of dunking new crew members in the river here to ward off the spirits of the Highlands, about whom the Dutch —and Washington Irving—liked to tell stories. The treacherous winds whipping through the narrow Highlands often upset boats and frightened superstitious sailors into believing that maybe there was some truth in the Dutch legends. Sloops were constantly in danger in these waters during bad weather, and more than a few went down at World's End, where the river swerves to avoid West Point. The Hudson is deepest through these mountains and drops to more than 200 feet at World's End.

The passage through the Highlands is one of the most storied sections of the river; truth, fiction, and superstition are interwoven to produce a colorful Hudson mythology. More often than not, however, such stories reveal a good deal of folk humor.

As an Albany-bound steamer passed under Crow's Nest mountain one August evening, two gentlemen climbed the stairway from the saloon to the upper deck, spit cigar tips overboard, and stood admiring the scenery. After about an hour, one man began reeling in a gold chain about as long as his arm before finally producing from his pocket a great moon of a watch, which snapped open with authority to reveal its hands at half past eight. As he talked the man swung the watch around his finger a few times before it left his hand, arced out over the river, and made bull's-eye ripples where it hit the water. Strolling toward the stern his companion commented on the casual manner in which he had accepted the loss. "Aha! but it is *not* lost, sir. While you were looking overboard at the watch I notched the railing with my pen knife so that I know exactly where we were standing, and when we reach Albany I will have a deck hand go over the side to recover it."

The Poplopen Creek spills into the river near Fort Montgomery just north of Bear Mountain State Park. And not far south of there was the location for one of the most adventurous undertakings in Hudson Valley railroading, which failed before it reached the preliminary construction stages. Backers interested in linking the West Shore Railroad with points east of the river put forth a proposal for the formation of the Hudson Suspension Bridge & New England Railway. The roadbed for this complex venture was to have begun at water level and spiraled around the Dunderberg from Jones Point until it was high enough to cross the river at Anthony's Nose, where it would run toward New England. An 1891 river map shows the exact details of the route; the project's backers withdrew at the crucial stage of payment, however, and all that remains is the plan. But the Bear Mountain bridge is now suspended between solid rock faces at approximately the same location illustrated for the railroad span.

This old river map is also one of the few that show the location of what some think was the mythical village of Doodletown, up in the hills overshadowing Iona Island. It is difficult to find this tiny hamlet of a few houses and a school, and its origins and name have been mixed in controversy for years. When Revolutionary soldiers were defeated at forts Montgomery and Clinton, one story goes, the British played "Yankee Doodle" to goad the losers retreating through the mountains. Another version suggests that it was the retreating Yankees who piped patriotic songs as a gesture of defiance toward the British. The most plausible version, however, is that pursuing British troops rested on a plain while their bagpipers "doodled" on their doodlebags for the soldiers' entertainment. It is not difficult to suppose that a hamlet on the plain might thus be called Doodle-town; some residents in the vicinity swear, however, that they have never heard of the place.

The Hudson grows shallow as it flows past the Dunderberg and widens into Peekskill Bay. After the imagined ghosts of the High-lands, there are real ones: liberty ships anchored in the lee of the Dunderberg with battleship-gray paint peeling from their hulls as they ride in motionless uniformity. Across the channel, in direct contrast to these old-fashioned war veterans, is an atomic power plant for generating electricity. Structural-steel towers support high-voltage transmission lines strung across the river from the Indian Point plant, framing the view toward a gypsum-board factory on Haverstraw Bay.

After a dogleg bend at Peekskill, the Hudson narrows again be-tween Verplanck's and Stony Points, then becomes a meadow-wide waterway, expanding its shores to their greatest width, nearly three and a half miles. There, on the west bank of Haverstraw Bay not far from the old Grassy Point ferry slip, a marker designates the spot on Treason Hill where Benedict Arnold betrayed the United States and handed over sketches of West Point's fortifications to Major John André. André was captured with the evidence in Tarrytown but was confined for trial across the river in Tappan, southwest of Treason Hill. Beverly Robinson, a Tory whose Garrison house had been confiscated for Arnold's West Point headquarters, appealed to his friend George Washington to release André, but the General could not stay the execution order after a military trial and the English spy was hanged.

In sight of the Tappan Zee Bridge, the Piermont pier reaches almost halfway across toward the Hudson's east shore; in the nine-teenth century it provided a steamboat landing for Erie Railroad freight and passenger service. The shallow waters of the Tappan Zee reach, which provided a less expensive location for the Thruway bridge at Tarrytown, are also fished for shad as far down as the George Washington Bridge. Shad men from Hyde Park to the

Palisades agree that river fish are less popular today than they once were, and most blame real or imagined pollution in the river, where once oysters were cultivated.

More people live within the twenty-odd miles below the town of Piermont than along the entire river above, yet there is still a great deal of beauty along this stretch of the Hudson. To the south, the Palisades wall in the river's west shore for fifteen miles to the George Washington Bridge, which connects New Jersey with upper Manhattan. These sheer bluffs were called Weehawken by the Indians because the stone formations resembled tall, slender trees. An interstate park system has preserved this sliver of rugged beauty only a few miles from the millions of people who crowd into the stockade-like towers of Manhattan Island. Trails crisscross the rocky outcroppings and lead almost vertically down the several hundred feet to the water. From one vantage point Long Island Sound and the Whitestone and Throgs Neck bridges many miles to the east can be seen. The Palisades Interstate Parkway and the Henry Hudson Parkway are linked by the George Washington Bridge and carry much of Manhattan's commuter traffic; farther downtown the Lincoln and Holland tunnels pump automobiles into the city in the morning and drain them back to New Jersey during the evening rush hours. North of the maze of approach ramps for the Lincoln tunnel stands a monument marking the site where Alexander Hamilton was fatally shot in the duel with Aaron Burr. Not far away is the spot where Hamilton's son had been killed three years earlier in a similar defense of his honor. The heights overlooking the Hudson from the Hamilton monument swing down to the river where dry docks, scrap yards, container-ship docks and railroads vie for North River space.

The Hudson's east shore from Tarrytown to Yonkers is not as high nor as sheer as are the Palisades across the water. Many of the townships along this section of the river remain predominantly residential, catering to thousands of suburban businessmen whose working day begins with an hour's commuting by rail to Wall Street. This western edge of Westchester County is hemmed in by the Penn Central's Hudson Division, which bends inland at Sputyen Duyvil, where the Harlem River joins the Hudson. The land continues to be uneven and hilly past the Cloisters, the tenements of Harlem, Grant's Tomb, Riverside Church, and the great walls of residences along Riverside Drive. Below Sixtieth Street piers jut into North River like whiskers, and fringe Manhattan with berths for the great ships of the world. The East River connects Long Island Sound with the Hudson estuary at the Battery. Diagonally across upper New York Bay the Kill Van Kull provides an outlet for Newark Bay and a channel for tankers headed for refineries at Bayonne or any one of a number of fuel-storage tank farms along the western reaches of Staten Island. Below the Kill Van Kull the Hudson passes the hour-glass neck of the Narrows and flows under the Verrazano Bridge into Lower Bay. It does not stop at land's end, however, but continues on to deepen a trench in the ocean floor for more than a hundred miles until it becomes indistinguishable from the sea.

From the Adirondacks to the Ambrose Light at its mouth, Hudson's River entices people to its shores and enchants them with its variety, power, and beauty. The river is a snare for the curious; it draws men into its sphere and works on their spirits. For some, of course, it is only what keeps the ferry from sinking, but for those who work and navigate its waters the Hudson is more than just a river. It is a way of life.

THREE

MARK TWAIN once said that a steamboat pilot on the Mississippi had to know the river as well as he knew his own front parlor in the dark, and the same kind of intuitive maneuvering still determines the success of a Sandy Hook or Hudson River pilot. More or less assured that the furniture will be kept in place from day to day, a pilot memorizes the Hudson's floor, all its obstacles, and how to avoid them. He can guide Day liners through the narrow passage at World's End or keep a cement barge off the mud flats in Esopus meadows with the certainty of a man walking barefoot past the piano without the lights on. The mechanical advantages of radar and automatic warning buoys are helpful but cannot replace human judgment in safe navigation. When two large tankers meet in what old sailors called The Race, the swift, wind-whipped current off Iona Island, only skillful handling and calm commands keep these oilers apart. Without Sandy Hook and Hudson River pilots, there would be chaos in tidewater shipping, and without the assurance of safe passage the commercial strength of the river would be less than assured.

But upriver traffic, once so variegated, has dwindled in a generation to only a few types of ships, which carry mostly stone products and fuel oil. In an age when technical leeway in marine design would permit construction of almost any kind of river craft, it is ironic that shipping on the Hudson has decreased rather than expanded. These days, however, planners ignore the river. Men look elsewhere for wealth and those who doggedly hang on discover that trying to make a living from the river itself is hopeless. The men who still go out in boats to fish are resigned to the inevitable.

Naawah, there's plenty of sturgeon in the river, always has been; they've ruined at least one net a year on me ever since I started fishin'. Trouble is, they don't just go through yer net and put a hole in it; they play wit' the damn thing, tear it in a lotta places.

Shure they're big! A cow'll go three, maybe four, hundred pounds. Depends. But you see nobody wants 'em anymore. Don't pay. I don't even bother to take a license.

The shad run is none too good these days neither. Market's down; people believe they can taste oil from the river. Maybe they can. Though it's probably kerosene that guys spill in their boats and don't bother cleanin' up. Striped bass on the other hand is as good eatin' as shad, I personally think better, and ya don't have the bones, but when a woman comes down to buy shad she won't try nothin' else. I can't figure it, women.

Lotta herring in the river lately, but you can't get nobody to spend time fix'n thum. You can eat smoked herring like peanuts; 'course you might like to take a drink too.

That boat there is over a hundred years old. My father built it. Probly's had a half-million fish in it over the years, maybe more, maybe less, you know what I mean? I put the new seat in it last season.

Tankers? Well, it's all accordin' to how they feel. Yeah, they're supposed to go around, but supposin' to and going around are two different things, and there's no way in the world you can argue. Sometimes a guy'll come out by the rail and curse his head off, but he figures it's either him or me, and there's not much chance of it bein' him. Oh, I guess I can see his point all right; it's either avoid me an' put her on the rocks or not avoid me, and I can tell ya not too many's been outta that channel.

Down near Oss'ning they use stake nets because the river's not too deep and it's wide enough so that they can fish and not get'n the waya boats. Up here we use drift nets, fishin' forty, forty-five feet deep, and a tanker will ride right over yer net, but they churn up the bottom, and that's no good either. Towboats don't sit so low in the water, but they'll foul into yer net or suck it up somehow, and that'll be the end of it, never find it again. They don't all do it, only some of thum, but we don't waste our time reportin'.

Hell, whataya gonna do?

For most old-timers, fishing in the Hudson River has not been very profitable since the Korean War. Professional fishing is now down to a minimum, and a few more men drop out each year. Most cannot support themselves on their catches, but shad men continue to fish "just one more year," hoping for a good season and trying to break even in the spring market. Trawlers still return to their home ports in New York harbor, bringing sea catches to Fulton Street markets, but the take from the upriver Hudson is paltry at its very best. There are areas of the river where pollution has virtually elimi-nated all fish, yet fish were once one of the river's great attractions. In the very early days of discovery and settlement along the Hudson River fish were a necessity for survival. The river teemed with a huge variety, and its pure waters provided the natural surroundings for species that have long since disappeared. Food fish from the river are not vigorously advertised anymore, and most of the fresh shad sold in New York now comes from the Delaware, but there was a time when Dutchmen came to take fish from the river, and many remained to live by its shores.

On April 26, 1640, city planner and prophet David DeVries sailed his *sloëp* across Newburgh Bay until twilight forced him to anchor off Danskammer Point. It was customary for Lenape and Wappingers Indians to unburden their spirits with a good deal of gyrating hocus-pocus on this rock plateau, and the early Dutch began calling this promontory the "devil's dance chamber." Silhouetted against the afterglow, the Indians' riotous behavior was certainly noticed by DeVries, who posted the ship's company on guard and decided that this was not a likely area for settlement. Upriver at the mouth of Rondout Creek the following day, he saw land that the Indians had cleared for corn, and in the vicinity of Catskill "savages" were at work planting. Rensselaerwyck was a tiny cluster of buildings with a hint of expanding into a village at the time of DeVries' visit, with "farms all around and every peasant a trader." After almost a month in the Albany district, during which this Dutch "explorer" penetrated as far as the Cohoes Falls, he retraced his route toward Staten Island and later filed a report that the river banks were "all stony and hilly," which he judged to be "unfit for dwellings." He noted that the tide ran all the way to the "colonie of Beverwyck" but that the land along the river was generally "little fitted to be people." DeVries was not the last to misjudge the potential in the river valley, nor was he the first to suggest that the Hudson was a commercially navigable waterway.

Hudson River ferries were simple in the beginning, carrying makeshift sail arrangements in addition to manpower. In time the newer ferries adopted the "improved" horse- or mule-driven treadwheel design. These early boats varied in size, but practically none could carry more than two or three wagons and a handful of animals at a time. It was not uncommon for the wagons or carriages to be unhitched and the teams forced to swim behind the ferry. The rate schedules at these crossings varied as much as the tides, and it was advisable to read the fine print in the advertisements. Rates were subject to change according to season, river location, or the ferry operator's choler at the time. A single passenger's fare was simple to reckon, but there were other, more complicated rates. At Hudson, for example, there was a fairly standard rate for daytime crossings. If, however, passage was necessary before the normal day's run began or after it had ended, then there was an additional fee, which increased if river conditions forced the boat owner to go around the flats off Hudson's dock. A rider and horse—or a rider and horse with one additional riderless animal—could expect an interesting bargaining session with the ferryman. A rider and horse with carriage and additional riderless animals, simply had to come to terms before the trip began. But there was always the consolation that a wagon team could swim behind the ferry at no additional charge.

Ferry lines prospered spasmodically; some crossings were absorbed or eliminated by competition a few miles away. The ferries were usually ten or fifteen miles apart, but there were instances in which competitors worked the same locations. Changes in interior routing often eliminated small lines or prompted establishment of new crossings. The ferry at Albany was an important railroad connection in the nineteenth century, and commerce from Connecticut was funneled across the Fishkill plains to the landing for Newburgh. In fact the ferry line there outlasted all other upriver service, succumbing only to the Newburgh-Beacon Bridge in 1963, to end a colorful era in Hudson River history. Ferry lines had prospered and decayed with the times, but, regardless of inefficiency or whim, they had given good service to the people of the valley.

If cornered and advised on the secret of successful business enterprise, a young eighteenth-century river man would have heard the golden word "sloops." Sloops were "in" almost from the start. In fact they were so important a part of river traffic that they did not disappear until well over half a century after steamers were in common use. Between the exploration by the *Half Moon* in 1609 and the successful New York-Albany round trip of Robert Fulton's *Clermont* in 1807 the sloop came of age and flourished.

The Hudson River sloop evolved until it was in general use, with fewer and fewer variations. The typical sloop was between sixty-five and eighty feet long, with a cargo capacity of about 100 tons. The mast was well forward, giving the advantage of a large mainsail and a small jib. The bowsprit was fixed, and very early a centerboard, sometimes called a "shifting keel," was introduced to prevent running aground in mud flats or shoal waters. No great science was needed to construct one of these early models, and it was not until shipyards began to attract skilled carpenters that sloop construction became a craft.

When running before the wind a sloop could reach speeds of up to twelve or fifteen miles an hour. The sloop *Caroline* once beat sixty miles up the river from New York to Fishkill Landing in five hours. This trip was made, of course, with favorable wind and tide, two very important considerations. With a good breeze a sloop could beat to windward against the tide and rough, choppy water was no problem if the boat had sufficient weight. But if the wind and tide were both unfavorable sloops—and most other tide-water sailing vessels—had to wait as long as six hours at anchor until the tide changed. With an ebb tide and a stiff wind blowing down the Race, as many as fifty to a hundred ships could collect in Peekskill Bay waiting for the flood. It was a forest of slender masts bunched at the southern gateway to the Highlands, and captains were able to trade shipping news or gossip or boast of their speed until the tide changed. Then there would be a mass exodus upstream, and the forest would thin out as the faster sloops led the line north.

The tides were of the greatest consideration to sloop captains, and their many peculiarities had to be thoroughly understood for a successful river career. In many parts of the river the flood runs as strong as the ebb most of the year, with some variations in spring and fall. During a wet spring fresh-water tributaries and the force of the upper Hudson itself slow the flood about twenty miles south of Albany, so that its only effect there is on the water level. The salt content in tidewater Hudson is neutralized before the flood reaches New York City's pumping station at Chelsea, and variation in strength is determined by the amount of precipitation during the year. With the spring freshets and normal rainfall, the flood tide carries salt water no farther north than Newburgh. After one particularly dry summer, ocean water penetrated farther north than normal, resulting in an influx of fresh-water fish just ahead of the salt line. Naturalist John Burroughs recalled that people from Poughkeepsie were able to chop holes in the ice that winter and casually scoop fish out of the river at will.

Passenger travel by sloop could be as interesting as an individual cared to make it, since, in many instances he was responsible for his own bedding, food, utensils, and, if he had livestock, animal feed. Larger, better-equipped sloops had accommodations in the stern for passengers or the captain's family. A voyage from an upriver landing to Old Slip in New York City might be talked about for years.

The packet sloop *Mohawk* tacking along the Palisades in a painting by Pavel Petrovich Svinin (1787–1839) (*New York Public Library, New York City*)

Sloops designed for passenger accommodations had room only for light parcels and mail in their freight holds. Certain captains developed reputations and followings because of the no-nonsense dispatch of their ships. Packages and letters were sent upriver on favorite sloops with trusted captains rather than risk the loss of property or time with unknown or forgetful seamen. The captain brought the news and mail and frequently made much better time in the warm seasons than the stagecoach did on its best days.

A great many Hudson River sloops combined freight and passenger service or were built specifically for the profits in hauling. The captain was a respected citizen in his community and acted as a middleman between rural and urban interests. Hudson River farmers shipped their produce to New York markets via sloop and were paid according to the success of the captains' bargaining technique. The sloop captain received a percentage of the total sale, thus ensuring the farmer a fair price. On the return trip to tidewater landings a sloop would carry manufactured items for upriver consumers or raw materials for businesses along the river.

When packet sloops could no longer compete for passengers with steamboats and the new Hudson River Railroad, they turned to carrying a variety of cargoes. In addition to coal from the Delaware & Hudson canal at the Rondout, they carried bricks, lime, cement, bluestone, lumber, flagstone, pig iron, cattle, vegetables, slate, grain, dead hogs, sheep, and cotton for the mills on the Fishkill and Wappingers creeks. Sloops also carried on trade with the West Indies, shipping livestock and returning with molasses, but this island trade was not extensive or durable, because a sloop's capacity did not permit profits in proportion to the required effort and time at sea. The *Clermont* and the subsequent proliferation of steamboats did not immediately eliminate the sloop; it died only after the appearance of large tows: barges, scows, and canal boats, sometimes as many as fifty, drawn along by one or two steamboats. Sloops were usually faster than tows but less dependable, and it was not uncommon to see one of these becalmed sailboats tied alongside a barge. Once towboat companies were able to offer larger capacities for upriver commerce, combined with reasonable speed and regularity, sails on the Hudson were doomed. As profits fell some sloops were redesigned and their riggings altered to convert them to schooners. Another mast and more sails could be added to a sloop, and frequently it was lengthened to provide better handling or to permit larger capacities. New schooners were also built at Haverstraw, Grassy Point, Tomkins Cove, Newburgh, Kingston, Tivoli, Catskill, Coxsackie, and Albany.

The *Greene County Tanner,* out of Catskill, was built in 1832, twenty-five years after the *Clermont's* first run to Albany. The *Tanner,* as its name implies, began service carrying hides from the Greene County tanneries, which used processed bark from the hemlock forests in the area until the trees were practically eliminated. After that flagstone and bluestone became *Tanner's* main cargoes. It was the captain of the *Tanner* who brought the first shocking news of President Lincoln's assassination to many river men, although most people in the Hudson valley received word by wire, via the railroad, or from passengers disembarking from New York steamboats. The speed of other means of communication obviated the river captains' function of "spreading the news." Within ten years after Lincoln had died, sloop and schooner captains ended their sailing careers; steam was in its heyday.

A little after noon on August 18, 1807, a gentleman pushed inward through the swinging doors of Jacques's Tavern, in Rhinecliff, and after slugging down a drink on the house to calm himself, related to all assembled that he had just seen "the devil going up the river on a sawmill." He had another drink. What he had seen was the *Clermont* belching smoke and fire as it proceeded toward Albany. Thurlow Weed, the politician, tells in his autobiography how, in order to have a good look at the *Clermont,* he and a friend floated their clothes on boards and swam out to an island in the middle of the river a day or two before the steamboat passed; it was so close "you could almost spit on the bow."

If all who later claimed to have seen the *Clermont's* maiden voyage had actually been lined up on shore, Fulton would have been unable to see the landscape. But the trip *was* a popular event, and sizable crowds stood on the Manhattan dock to cheer or jeer Fulton as he backed out into the harbor on his tiny steamer—rigged with a sail just in case something went wrong. After a half-hour delay for

Robert Fulton's *Clermont* begins its historic voyage up the Hudson in 1807. (*Courtesy of The New York Historical Society, New York City*)

repairing what did go haywire, Fulton headed for Albany and a fortune for having successfully developed a feasible method using steam to drive a vessel forward through the water. Robert Fulton, artist, civil engineer, scientist, and inventor, was perhaps most important of all an optimist. It was his belief in himself and his knowledge of steam as a motive power—combined with the moral and financial support of Chancellor Livingston, his partner and cousin by marriage that enabled him to take the devil up the river on a sawmill with the entire shipping world reeling behind.

Steam was in! Steam ferrys, steamboats, tugboats, and freighters all competing, converging on the river in one grand melee of power, elegance, utility, and speed. The Fulton-Livingston team for a time had exclusive rights to all steamboat traffic on the river. Only after Daniel Webster had successfully argued the case against their monopoly before the U.S. Supreme Court did the great boom really begin; then the lid blew off shipping like the first corks after the repeal of Prohibition. The Day Line, the Night Line, the People's Line, the North River Line, and other companies exploded into the business of carrying passengers and freight from one end of tidewater Hudson to the other. The competition was incredible. Each company overhauled its boats during the winter in order to meet the next season with lengthened keels, new decking, promenades, dining rooms, cabins, and bars. The interiors were redecorated, and increased profits one year meant larger ships the next. Many steamboats were enlarged simply by sawing off the bows and adding a few more feet of lumber. Some ships lost their graceful proportions during these remodeling seasons, but others suffered very little under the weight of new extras. Even a calliope was installed in one steamer, to attract new customers, but it had a tendency to irritate the passengers and used more steam than was practical for the ship's efficient operation.

Despite the popular preoccupation with speed, the Hudson River steamboat was not without elegance and charm. The ships also provided one of the finest means of transportation that men had yet devised. Steamboats varied in size, design, accommodations, and beauty. Almost all were painted white, with names lettered across their drum-like paddle boxes. Most had three passenger decks, but a few, like the People's liner *C. W. Morse,* had four, with an observation room on the top, or hurricane deck. Smokestacks were amidships, usually behind the walking beam in the center of a cluster of ventilation funnels. From six to a dozen poles flying American, state, or company flags lined the upper deck behind the wheelhouse, and countless thousands of travelers sunned themselves under these flapping banners.

Interior appointments were plush and well cared for during the good years, from the 1870s through the 1890s. The floors were carpeted, the walls paneled in mahogany, and the ceilings hung with gilded lamps. Armchairs were arrayed along a passage with long rows of windows in front and large murals of river views or scenes from Rip Van Winkle on the walls behind. One of the most unusual touches of luxury on any steamboat was the ornate Alhambra design of the writing room in the saloon of the *Washington Irving.* Carved paneling and pillars surrounded letter writers with a Moorish atmosphere as they addressed any one of a series of Hudson River foldout postcard booklets that was very popular around the turn of the twentieth century.

The engine rooms were kept as spotless as the upper decks, and highly polished brass fittings blinded bystanders who came to watch engineers turn down grease cups while the engines were still running. When interest in the engine was no longer overpowering, a bystander might stare at the incomprehensible operations of the steam-steerage motor that was encased in glass on many boats. Most passengers, however, crowded the decks and watched the uneven hills of the Hudson disappear astern.

The boat-building industry thrived again in Hudson River towns from Watervliet to Hoboken and improved; more commodious models were built each year. Boat companies did not always stop at the same landings, and there was a variety of schedules and routes up and down the river. Some dayboats ran upstream only as far as Peekskill, others to the Rondout Creek. Longer routes caromed from shore to shore all the way to Albany, and companies provided daily service in each direction. Passenger vessels did not carry heavy freight but limited cargoes to light parcels, mail, baggage and coal for the boilers. Freight boats, designed for fast service, carried movable cargoes and commodities were shipped by scow or canal boat. Tow-boat companies were established, and the Swift Sure Line bought a fleet of steam tugs for safety-barge operations, which were popular in the years immediately after the opening of the Erie canal in 1825.

The safety barge was a boat designed to eliminate exploding boilers and steamboat fires. It was a "dry" vessel, carrying no boilers or similar explosive hazards. It had no motive power of its own but was usually towed at the end of a fifty-yard hawser. Some were much closer to the tug or steamboat, for they could also be connected by a gangway on a floating swivel. In the event of a fire or boiler explosion on a towboat, the barge was in danger only from falling debris, and even the swivel gangway could be cast off from the tug. The safety barges carried freight, provided meals, and offered overnight accommodations. They provided slow transportation, despite company names, but women brought their uncut books, men smoked in a special room, and everyone listened to animals moaning in the holds.

There are no modern equivalents to the old tows. Today a dozen steel barges at most are drawn in pairs by a single powerful diesel tug. Although the number of barges in modern tows is much smaller, the overall capacity is as great or greater than the earlier "sea trains." The old, long, heavy-looking tows took hours to pass out of sight, and a vegetable man in a bumboat could take advantage of this leisurely pace to sell fresh garden produce to each barge captain's wife. But a diesel tug can now push a barge more than 100 yards long from the Port of New York to Albany in less than twenty-four hours. These tugs are big, automated, and easy to handle. Thirty years ago it took as many as a dozen to dock enormous liners like the *Queen Elizabeth* or the *Ile de France,* but today similar ships are pushed and pulled into North River piers by half that number, all under the skillful direction of a single docking pilot. He is usually a senior tugboat captain who climbs aboard ship before it hoves to off its particular pier. These ships may be drawing from twenty to thirty-five feet of water and can be affected by four or five different tide and current conditions simultaneously. The river's surface may be at slack tide while ten feet below a slight flood is still running. Ten feet below that the water might be beginning to ebb. Wind is another extremely important factor, and a docking pilot must know exactly when to cut the ship's main engines as he signals commands to his tugs on a police whistle. Once the liner is warped to the pier, its deep-throated whistle blasts a release to the tugboats. The docking pilot may then button his jacket, tighten his tie, climb down onto his tug, and prepare to pick up a junk barge in New Jersey.

Oil and gasoline were not popular river commodities in the days of the long tows, and when they did become important they were transported in railroad tank cars. Now most bulk petroleum shipments go upriver in tankers or a pair of scows that can carry from 30,000 to 100,000 barrels each. Ocean-going tankers have such large capacities these days, however, that some fully laden ships cannot run all the way to Albany. Many oilers do not tie up at docks anymore either but unload at small pipeline piers, which jut into the river from large holding tanks.

Steel hulls and powerful engines have also made seasonal shipping in the tidewater Hudson a thing of the past. The barge canals are closed in winter, but the U.S. Coast Guard stations icebreakers in the lower Hudson to keep tidewater navigation open. In winter the river ice becomes a class in geometry. When icebreakers split fissures in the solid cake, triangles, rectangles, squares, parallelograms, and now and then rhombuses appear. These geometric figures pile up one another in a giant jigsaw puzzle, driven by relentless tidal pressure, as well as being buffeted by wind and current. Transcendentalists might be interested in fitting the broken pieces into a universal plan, but practical yacht clubs along the tidewater Hudson drag their ramps in before December or build new ones in late March.

The Coast Guard ships *Mahoning, Manitou, Sauk, Sassafras,* and *Red Beech* have been maintaining the shipping channel in recent years, but when the ice grows more than two feet thick—and it does—the larger, polar icebreakers are dispatched for Hudson River duty. The channel ice that is broken up during the day refreezes at night so that the whole process must be repeated again and again. Ship captains say that there is nothing certain about cutting ice on the Hudson because conditions vary along the tidewater and can be quite different from year to year. Chunks of ice piled under pressure into windrows are the most difficult obstacles, especially in the West

Point area, where the river narrows and tremendous jams occur. Then the Coast Guard captain runs his ship up onto the ice with the aid of specially designed, reinforced bow so that its great weight can crush the jam. This slow, back-and-forth movement is tedious work that some seamen find difficult to adjust to, but it is an important duty to keep the channel open for vital fuel deliveries. Hudson River shipping is limited in winter, but nevertheless a steady stream of oilers push frozen prows through the ice, helping to keep the channel passable. This traffic was not possible seventy-five years ago, and men came down to the river to take advantage of the ice industry's winter harvests.

The Knickerbocker Ice Company was about the largest concern to cut ice from the Hudson and from many fair-sized lakes between New York and Albany. Special tools (many of which are now on the bottom) were used by teams of men and horses that worked long hours to fill huge poll barns on the hills over the river. There the large blocks were packed in sawdust until the summer months, when they were sent down chutes to fill barges headed for the greater New York City market. The barges were strung behind tugs or old steamboats, which in their later years could no longer compete in the passenger trade. Some old steamers were rebuilt as towboats, but others were used in deteriorating condition until they could no longer be operated profitably. They were eventually phased out of freight hauling just as they had been eliminated from the glamor and excitement of the passenger trade.

Steamboat travel in the early years was infectious, and people boarded vessels who might never have stepped off the dock had they known what a trip up the river could be like. If they were not apprehensive in the beginning they had good reason to show concern after reputations for recklessness became well known. Racing steamboats was more than a sport among captains, who sought with ruthless vigor to maintain or achieve dominance. Passenger safety was of little concern when the race was on, and many travelers were scalded to death or drowned when boats exploded and sank. Safety valves on boilers were often tied down and the ships allowed to run full-out in an effort to pass rivals or to stay ahead of them. Steamboats often skipped landings in order to gain or keep the advantage in a race, and on one occasion passengers demanding to get off at a particular town were put over the side of the ship in a small rowboat, which promptly sank, drowning all its occupants in the wash of the steamboat as it pulled away.

Arguments among captains over the relative merits of certain steamboats were often carried as far as the company managements, which feuded with one another anyway. Daniel Drew, Commodore Cornelius Vanderbilt, Charles Morse, Jim Fisk, Chauncey Vibbard, and a few other steamship executives had been hacking away at one another for years. It did not matter whether they fought for ship lines or railroads; the struggle was the same, and ruthless ground rules prevailed.

Much of the competition for river monopolies also filtered down from corporate offices to the actual operators of the steamboats and the people who rode on them. Gimmickry and fraud were used to great advantage during these battles for control, but most passengers were unaware that there was anything more to steamboating than going up and down the Hudson. Passengers jamming the piers and about to board one steamboat were induced by ticket hawkers to take other boats for less. Price wars were strenuously fought, and some companies were not above pirating passengers from other ships, or kidnapping them from the streets. Even occasional bystanders were known to make the Albany round trip after being grabbed by mistake. One lady in New York fell for a hawker's line and boarded a sidewheeler only after being assured that the boilers could not explode, for, as her luck would have it, this particular ship did not carry any. Undercutting the competition did not involve only lowering fares; free meals and sleeping accommodations were also included. Steamboat companies slugging it out for passengers at one time drove the one-way fare to Albany down to about 10 cents, but this had to stop when no one backed down, and a truce was declared in order for the lines to remain within the bounds of economic realism.

The kind of thing that irritated Cornelius Vanderbilt was the league that Daniel Drew formed with the New York Central. Vanderbilt's Hudson River Railroad and the New York Central had only the Albany steamer docks in common, and each company did what it could to harass the other whenever an occasion presented itself. Daniel Drew's People's Line was on the best of terms with the New York Central, and much of the railroad's western freight arriving in Albany was shipped on Drew liners rather than over Vanderbilt's railroad. In 1867 the New York Central absorbed the Saratoga & Hudson River Railroad and then connected with the People's Line steamer at Athens. This move enabled the Central to bypass Albany altogether providing direct steamboat passenger service from its Athens station to New York City. The Day Line also neglected its Hudson landing for a time, in order to take advantage of the through traffic at Athens. But this scheme to foster a new passenger route was a failure, and the Saratoga & Hudson River line became popularly known as the "White Elephant Railroad"; even freight service was finally discontinued.

Vanderbilt smarted for years from Drew's stock-market manipulations and other schemes to cut down the Commodore wherever possible. But Vanderbilt retaliated for wounds inflicted by the White Elephant Railroad project, eventually acquiring the prosperous New York Central himself. This merger with the Hudson River line was a severe blow to the steamboat business on the Hudson and also did considerable economic damage to the Erie canal system, which had been hard pressed enough trying to keep pace with just the New York Central. The creation of a direct rail route from New York City to Buffalo was a signal advance in long-haul transportation, and the canal-river link had to cope with the realities of progress.

The Erie canal was opened in 1825, after years of planning problems, political in-fighting, and construction difficulties. The prime mover was De Witt Clinton, who was on board the *Seneca Chief*, the boat that led the first speech-making, flag-waving flotilla through the canal toward Cohoes. At the Hudson the steamer *Chancellor Livingston* took the *Seneca Chief* in tow, and the celebration fleet sailed for Lower Bay and the symbolic "wedding of the waters," during which a cask of Lake Erie water was poured into the Atlantic Ocean. A feature of these opening celebrations was a cannon salute marking the beginning of the *Seneca Chief*'s journey. Cannon were positioned within sound range of one another across the whole state and down the Hudson valley, ready to relay the signal from the lakes to the Port of New York, a kind of gunpowder version of the Indian smoke signal. It took more than two hours to be transmitted to New York and returned.

New York City manufacturers and merchants were pleased with the canal; shipping companies were happy with the new barge traffic; agricultural and urban interests all across the central portion of the state looked toward a promising future—but the Hudson River valley farm belt was severely shaken by the devastating competition from the Mohawk frontier.

A number of "port" cities across the state trace their origins directly to the construction of the Erie route. The canal system also stimulated expansion of related industries in Hudson River towns and served as a main migration route to the Midwest. Mainly Irish labor was exploited in the construction of the Erie and its lateral connections. These men were paid $1 a day but had to spend it in company stores that made anywhere from 100 to 150 percent profit. These immigrant laborers were brought to this country in exchange for work commensurate with the cost of passage. The one-way fare seemed to take forever to erase, and Irish slang for the company deal referred to it as "working off the dead horse." Indians were also employed in the early building of the Erie, and there is no reason to believe that they were treated any better than the Irish. Canal work was one of the few areas in which Irish applications were readily accepted. In 1862 the canal was enlarged until its prism was seventy feet on the surface, seven feet deep, and fifty-six wide on the bottom. This larger channel made possible an increase in the capacity of a single canal boat to more than 350 tons, and profits continued to climb. New York City received a considerable share of Erie profits, for the waterway west gave the city an important trade advantage over other seaboard rivals.

The construction of the Erie and its lateral canals during the first quarter of the nineteenth century triggered interest in canal building all over the state. The Champlain canal and the Glens Falls feeder were built simultaneously with the Erie. The year "Clinton's ditch" was opened the privately owned and operated Delaware & Hudson Canal Company began digging its 107-mile route from Honesdale, Pennsylvania, to the Rondout Creek at Kingston. This canal was primarily for carrying coal and operated, mostly prosperously, until 1899. Towboat companies were established at the mouth of the Rondout to haul the coal boats south. Similar companies operated out of Cohoes and Albany. These days traffic on the Rondout has been reduced to carrying stone products, but barges, now made of steel, are still launched sideways into the creek, as they have been since the days of the Delaware & Hudson.

When engineers laid out the route from Honesdale to Kingston, they discovered that the Wallkill-Rondout region along the canal had great deposits of high-grade aggregate for the cement industry. Consequently, the mountains near Kingston were, and still are, tapped to provide the adhesive for half of New York City. Cement from around Rosendale west of Kingston became famous for its weather-resistant quality and was used exclusively in the construction of the Brooklyn Bridge. Not too many years ago, when the bridge was repointed, a Rosendale plant was reopened to provide the necessary cement because of its unique quality. The D & H canal carried a good deal of cement to the tidewater Hudson before low profits and railroads forced it out of business. Trees now grow in the abandoned locks, and traces of the old towpaths can be seen here and there all the way to Honesdale.

In 1918 statewide expansion of the toll-free canal system was completed. The channels followed the rivers and lake beds wherever possible, and diesel engines replaced mules or horses. But the state barge canals are used commercially today only for bulk cargoes. The competitive railroads, which forced many private barge and steamboat owners out of business, have increased their efficiency, while the barge canals continue to slip into obsolescence. The area railroads, which fought for patronage in Albany, have now merged into the largest rail-transportation complex in the country. They cart coal trains intact from the Pennsylvania fields and have other specially built cars that can be put directly aboard ships without having to be unloaded. River shipping is now managed scientifically by computers, which load and unload cargo as well as keeping track of where a company's floating stock is and where it should be at any given time. New barge designs and construction materials have increased the versatility of this kind of shipping, but the volume of

Hudson River commercial traffic is ebbing. Few look to the river as a trade artery anymore, and towns that were once caught up in the business of the Hudson no longer find it relevant.

It has been twenty years since the Day Line's *Robert Fulton* ended service to Albany, and the company now has no upriver landings north of West Point. The only Hudson River steamboat of the old class (design only) still in operation is the *Alexander Hamilton,* and this sidewheeler rarely goes north of Poughkeepsie's old Continental Shipyards anymore. Highways and railways have wooed traffic away from the river, and there are times now when the Long Reach, the Ditch, and the Tappan Zee are empty. It seems impossible that after 300 years of navigation the Hudson River should be commercially obsolete, but, ironically, that is what it is.

FOUR

A COMMUTER traveling south on the Hudson division of the old New York Central looked through the rain on the window one morning and saw a red-nosed jet sucking in air about fifty feet above the river. He had never seen that type of plane so close to the water before, and it seemed about to make an emergency landing. Just as the commuter roused the man to his left and pointed toward the jet, their local entered the Breakneck Ridge tunnel, and the whole scene was blacked out. When the lights came up again, the jet was almost as high as Storm King Mountain and beginning to heel over toward the west. The man in the next window seat forward raised his head and explained.

"Every now and then," he said, "you see one of those jets sneaking up the Hudson to avoid the radar at Stewart Air Force Base just over the hill there behind Newburgh. Pilots go through simulated attacks to keep the spotters alert and occasionally the base scrambles some interceptors into the air. That is, I *assume* it was one of *our* planes."

Stewart Field, the base's popular name, was originally the Newburgh city airport, a tract of 172 acres conveyed to the city for $1 by Samuel Stewart in honor of his father, Lachlan Stewart, with the provision that the field retain the family name. The base is now more than ten times as large as when Newburgh bought it, and training missions have been conducted there ever since the United States acquired the air strip in October 1935. Big Globemaster transports ferry supplies in and out of Stewart, keeping reserve pilots proficient. It is not uncommon for men from Stewart's supply wing to fly war material to Vietnam in a new kind of Red Ball express, leaving the base on Fridays and returning three days and about 20,000 miles later. Since World War II men from Stewart have served in all American wars and crises. Situated in mountain folds not far from where George Washington once rejected a proposal to make him king, Stewart has beefed up its defensive arm and is today one of the important air bases in the East.

After acquisition by the Federal government, the base was used as a training field for air cadets from the U.S. Military Academy and in 1941 became part of West Point. As flight training expanded, the Federal government acquired auxiliary fields in the Hudson valley region at Montgomery, Wallkill, and New Hackensack. These small airfields were used as practice strips for takeoff, landing, and touch-and-go maneuvers. Flying instruction was seriously considered at West Point after World War I but because of limited facilities training continued to be limited in those years to the lecture hall. Actually, as early as 1915 General Maxwell Van Zant Woodhull had argued in his critical and prophetic study of the Academy *West Point in Our Next War,* that it was essential for the army to get hold of "aeroplanes" and hydroplanes and to allow interested cadets to make two or three ascents a year.

In late 1927 an aircorps project with a half-dozen men and one Loening amphibian began using a new hangar and ramp on the Hudson River at West Point. It was aimed primarily at maintaining the proficiency of flying officers stationed at the Point. Eventually Academy interest in including aviation tactics in the curriculum had grown to the point at which authority to commission cadets in the air corps was granted. Stewart Field was enlarged, and a U.S. Army Air Force flying school was established with a detachment of more than 1,600 men. There were problems, however, primarily in coordination and the weather. Newburgh's sloping hillside, which Robert Juet had called "a good place to build a town," was in fact a good place for storms to cut through a gap in the mountains, with the result that it was often unsuitable for flying at Stewart at the same time that cadets started over Storm King from West Point under favorable skies. But the main problem was that there simply was not enough time to train cadets in both army and air-corps duties. As a result "wings" were awarded to West Point cadets for the last time in the 1946 graduating class. The Academy still participates in tactical courses at Stewart, but the emphasis at the base has now shifted to the air force and its ability to respond immediately with men and equipment for whatever job is required. The men stationed at Stewart train constantly to remain alert while on a hill above the acres of concrete runways a white puff-ball of a radar dome houses scanning equipment, which helps to guard against intrusions into American air space.

In 1775 the New York Provincial Congress kept itself well informed of British strategy on the Hudson and assumed the responsibility for providing appropriate counterplans and defenses. The Hudson's deep cut through the Highlands was ideal for a variety of defensive innovations and, if the river was to be protected at all, a good stand against the British could be made in these mountains. Preliminary fortification plans were drawn up and accepted by the Provincial Congress, which then ordered work begun on forts Montgomery and Clinton, which were to be built on each side of the Poplopen Creek.

Works were also to be thrown up on Fort Hill across from West Point. It was decided to string a chain-and-boom arrangement across the river, and Bernard Romans, a civil engineer from the Netherlands, was commissioned to direct the construction projects. In addition to Romans, several commissioners were appointed to expedite the construction directives from the Provincial Congress. Unfortunately opinions differed between the commissioners and Romans over the problems of authority, and out of this argument arose the more serious question of Romans' competence. He had chosen a spot at the bottleneck of the river, Fort Constitution, now Constitution Island, which could perhaps be useful in stopping advancing ships, but which also stretched out vulnerably under the shadow of the west point. Romans favored his Constitution site and ignored the high ground, which had the potential to command a much more tenable American position. If the west point were not fortified. British troops would need only to march over the mountains from behind, occupy the plain above the river, and render the Colonial armor at Fort Constitution impotent. Although works were ultimately thrown up on Constitution Island and Anthony's Nose, additional American surveys were also made in the Highlands between 1775 and autumn 1777, when English General Sir Henry Clinton launched his expeditionary move to break through rebel-controlled positions on the Hudson and eventually to rendezvous with General John Burgoyne at Albany.

On December 13, 1775, the Continental Congress made another significant military move, appointing a marine committee to plan and execute the construction and fitting out of warships. Thirteen ships were commissioned by the committee; they were to be built at several different locations. Two frigates were put on the ways at the Continental Shipyard in Poughkeepsie because of its relative security above the Highland fortifications and easy access to New England supplies. Before the summer of 1776 was over, General Washington had also ordered fire rafts built at Poughkeepsie, and fourteen had been launched by late July. In addition to this marine construction, which included the arming of sloops, blacksmiths near the Continental Shipyard were busy forging links to lengthen an iron chain sent down from Fort Ticonderoga to stretch across the river at Fort Montgomery. (About 100 years after the Revolution Poughkeepsie went from guns to butter when the famous DeLaval Cream Separator plant was opened in the vicinity of the shipyard.)

As November's somber grayness descended in 1776, sections of the new chain were hurriedly sent down to Fort Montgomery before the river froze over. The frigates were launched that same month. After spending the winter in the Rondout Creek for safety, they returned to the shipyard for fitting out and were deployed in the summer of 1777 to protect the chain at Fort Montgomery. A call also went out that summer for men to garrison forts Montgomery, Clinton, and

Constitution, but the response in Dutchess and Ulster counties was so disappointing that a commission was appointed to investigate the possibilities of conspiracy. Had the British known how poorly the Highlands were defended, they might well have proceeded upriver with little interference and possibly even averted Burgoyne's eventual defeat. Burgoyne's surrender at Saratoga in October 1777 and the failure to establish a British occupation force in the Highlands was a significant setback to English strategy if not the key to loss of the whole war. The British general staff had done its homework and had conceived a workable method for attacking the river valley, but squabbling among staff members and failures in communication marked the ultimate failure of the whole mission.

The royal plan was simple, sound, and not very original. Burgoyne presented it to His Majesty King George III during the winter of 1776 in a paper called *Thoughts for Conducting the War from the Side of Canada.* As finally determined, Burgoyne was to drive south from Montreal along Lake Champlain and the Hudson to Albany, where he would meet a column from General William Howe's army as it advanced up the Hudson from Manhattan; a small detachment of regulars would also march on the city from the Mohawk valley. Once the Hudson was secured, the New England colonies would be separated from the flow of men and supplies coming out of the South. This basic strategy could have worked, but the British somehow bungled this important phase of the war.

John Burgoyne began his march with more than 8,000 men, including Indians of the Six Nations and German infantrymen under Baron Friedrich Adolph von Riedesel. This force reached Fort Ticonderoga in a mammoth train of barges, bateaux, armed sloops, whaleboats, artillery carriers, and canoes all strung out for miles on Lake Champlain. The entire contingent was halted above the fort while siege cannon were floated ashore and positioned on a hill above the fort. American General Arthur St. Clair, who was in command of the garrison, was informed by scouts of Burgoyne's intrusion and, realizing the hopelessness of a long battle, escaped across the lake with his ill-supplied, invalid, and sick force of about 2,000 men. Burgoyne's force pursued St. Clair's army as it scattered into the hills but halted and regrouped after a few brief inconclusive skirmishes at Skenesboro and Fort Ann. The British had been successful, however, in terrorizing the unfortunate farmers caught in the line of march. Whole families hid in the nearby swamps, hoping to escape Burgoyne's men and murder by "those dreadful Indians." The farmers were surprised to find their homes and barns still standing when they returned—but they found nothing else. Crops, cattle, sheep, hogs, and horses were gone; anything useful and movable had disappeared.

An army traveling overland is in continual need of supplies, and instead of pressing directly toward Albany Burgoyne brought the main body of his attack force to a halt in order to forage the countryside and bolster his reserves. He was not unmindful of the well-stocked farming region to the east and decided that a brief foray into Vermont for food would not jeopardize the schedule for his main objective. But the dog days of summer were already over when General Burgoyne made this decision and sent Colonel Fredrick Baume and a contingent of Englishmen to raid the supply magazines at Bennington. The General expected Seth Warner's minutemen to be the only opposition to this venture, and he doubted that Warner's militia could stand against Baume.

Burgoyne's main force was by that time near forts Edward and Miller on the Hudson and had met little opposition, despite the violent indignation aroused in Americans by the senseless killing of Jane McCrea. One morning in early August, Burgoyne personally rode to Fort Miller with intelligence reports estimating that only 300 or 400 men were guarding the supplies at Bennington. He dispatched Baume's troops before more New England farmers could rally to Warner's call to arms. Burgoyne was, however, unaware that John Stark, a tall, lean veteran of Roger's Rangers and the French and Indian War, had already positioned his force at Bennington to protect the draught animals and other important provisions.

On August 14, 1777, Baume encountered a handful of the Bennington main force sent ahead to feel out his strength. After a brief skirmish he was encouraged to learn from prisoners that, although more men than he had anticipated waited at Bennington, they were nevertheless certain to bolt at their first taste of British fire power. But Baume's information was wrong; he had been tricked and was even led to believe that an advancing column of militiamen were, in fact, loyalists. One member of his force wrote later that "the rapid fire of musketry warned us to prepare for a meeting the reverse of friendly." Farmers behind Stark and Warner's reinforcements hacked at Burgoyne's mercenaries with staggering results. The English were routed, including the plodding, jackbooted Hessian support forces under the command of Colonel Heinrich von Breymann. The Bennington forces hit Burgoyne with both edges of the sword, inflicting more than 700 casualties and throwing into confusion the disgruntled Indians, Hessians, and redcoats, who were already on short rations. And there was still the question of Albany.

Revolutionary General Philip Schuyler had been making urgent demands for more troops as he plotted skillful retreat maneuvers before the advance of Burgoyne, who was by then camped above old Saratoga. General Israel Putnam dispatched Colonel John Nixon's Brigade to Albany by sloop and in mid-August ordered two more regiments also from the Highlands to join General Horatio Gates, who had superseded Schuyler. Before Gates took full command of the Northern Department, however, Schuyler gambled that Burgoyne's army would remain stationary and sent troops to halt the English drive through the Mohawk valley. He risked the Hudson to save the Mohawk—and won.

Burgoyne, though discouraged by the Bennington defeat, was still confident that Lieutenant Colonel Barry St. Leger would sweep down the Mohawk valley to Albany. But St. Leger was not meeting with the immediate and complete success he had expected. General Nicholas Herkimer, who was stationed in the Mohawk valley, had held up the British until St. Leger ambushed his army, then trapped him from behind with a combined force of Iroquois, English, and German soldiers. Herkimer was wounded, but by then Benedict Arnold, determined not to lose the Mohawk, was leading a force toward battle with St. Leger. As Arnold approached Fort Stanwix, where the British were camped, a fortunate set of circumstances enabled him to undermine the confidence of St. Leger's army. His success was predicated on knowledge of Indian superstition and the fear that might be planted in St. Leger's regulars.

Not far from Arnold's route lived John Joost Schuyler (no relation to General Philip Schuyler), Herkimer's nephew, who was thought to be half crazy. John Schuyler's family asked that he not be harmed, and Arnold agreed on condition that Schuyler, in return for his freedom, proceed to St. Leger's camp and, with all the gesticulations appropriate to a crazy man, relate the doom in store for the Indians if they fought against Arnold. (Indians were known to be afraid of the deranged.) An old sachem was also involved in the drama; he entered on cue to corroborate John Schuyler's story of the powerful American force that was advancing and that would show no mercy. Two more members of the cast, friendly Indians disguised as unfriendly Indian scouts, confirmed John Schuyler's report. These tactics were too much for many members of the Six Nations; words of an insane man were black omens. After a brief argument with St. Leger, who tried to get them drunk, most of the Indians fled into the woods—followed by the bulk of the English army.

Arnold discovered that St. Leger's retreat was, in fact, full flight. The English finally escaped across Oneida Lake, and St. Leger's phase of the British plan was effectively neutralized. Arnold's force rejoined the army at Albany to await Burgoyne's next move. As August drew to a close Johnny Burgoyne's fate was sealed. Howe wrote to congratulate him on his victory at Ticonderoga but expressed his own intention to press General Washington at Philadelphia. There was also little hope now that Clinton (with his lack of manpower and his poor communications with Burgoyne) could get upriver in time to meet Burgoyne with fresh forces unless new troops arrived from England on schedule. The alternatives open to the English army on the upper Hudson were now reduced to two. Burgoyne could either drive toward Albany by himself or pull back over the lake route to Canada. One thing was clear, however—it was time to move.

The military fortunes of General Horatio Gates had improved considerably in the last weeks of August, and he had already succeeded Schuyler as American Commander of the Northern Department when Arnold returned from the Mohawk. Arnold was a Schuyler man, and he and Gates had little use for each other but the General was a pragmatist and appointed the young fire-eater to command the left wing of his army. Gates held a strategy meeting in

Albany with all his officers except Schuyler and devised a plan to confront Burgoyne before he could proceed much farther south. The American army then moved north along the river and pushed inland at Bemis Heights, where the land forces road and river through a narrow passage. Thaddeus Kosciuszko, a young Polish engineer, chose this spot as the place to stop the British and at Gates' command began to lay out defenses and throw up works that would control the narrow valley below. About a half-mile inland from the Hudson the land sloped sharply upward to a very commanding position above the river.

In those days the road cut away from the base of the ridge and ran closer to the river. Both were in easy cannon range from the heights, and trees were felled to improve the field for shooting. Today a farm stretches between river and road, but the American redoubts are still discernible along the top of the ridge, now part of Saratoga National Historic Park. Metal maps show locations and importance of various defensive positions, and at the touch of a button an unseen speaker explains who was where and when and what happened. The landscape is not exactly the same today. The thick brush and trees that dominated much of it in September 1777 have to be imagined now. The river banks are still lined with trees, and distance deadens the sound of tugboats pushing lazily toward Albany and Troy. The scene is peaceful now, and summer bugs arc out of the grass where long ago horses were blown apart under their riders.

It was September 13, 1777, when Burgoyne ferried his army across to the west shore of the river at old Saratoga. If he continued down the east shore, the General reasoned, he would be forced to cross at Albany, where the river was wider, more dangerous, and thus more to the advantage of American gunners. Down the road that flanked the Hudson's west bank Burgoyne laboriously marched his train of men and equipment, as he waited for some feelers from Gates. Blindly he scanned the wooded ridges, but without his Indian scouts, who had deserted after the McCrea and Vermont episodes, he could discover no movement. Finally his forces arrived at the outer defenses of the Americans and were driven by artillery fire off the road into the heavy forests. There they heard wild-turkey calls, but they saw no turkneys; instead they found Dan Morgan's sharp-shooters, who picked them off one by one. The woods, thick and thatched with grapevines, made fighting difficult, and the battle moved into the cleared fields around Freeman's farm. The British army resolutely maintained attack formation, while Morgan's men took advantage of the scattered cover of the terrain. This first battle lasted only a day, and Burgoyne ordered his forces to pull back from the farm and to dig in to await Clinton's reserve troops. They did not come.

Three weeks went by while Burgoyne contemplated his next move. It was a difficult time for the British army. Harassed by sporadic fire during the night, the English and German soldiers slept armed and fully clothed. The tension of continual alerts made the men ornery and the officers quarrelsome. Men went hungry on half-rations, and horses died on no rations at all. On October 7 Bur-goyne decided that he could wait no longer and risked another en-gagement with Gates' now even larger force. In mid-afternoon a three-pronged American attack repeatedly broke through British lines, driving back the enemy. Simon Fraser, a popular English officer, was killed by a sharpshooter as he encouraged his infantry-men to stand and cover the diversionary maneuvers of other retreat-ing soldiers. The American forces nearly lost Benedict Arnold that same day. He had been relieved of his command after a procedural argument with Gates but had ignored the order and impetuously led the successful storming of a redoubt before being wounded in the leg. Had Arnold died in the trench, history would have given his name far different recognition. General Fraser was buried that night in the Great Redoubt, a large English earthenworks, while American artillerymen unknowingly shelled the British position. The following night Burgoyne's army retreated through the rain and took refuge in a fortified camp near Saratoga. There they were surrounded by 20,000 Americans, who cut off all roads of escape until Burgoyne finally surrendered.

A blindfolded English aide was brought to Gates with a message asking that fighting cease until Burgoyne could state his terms. Gates handed the officer his own terms for British surrender, thus opening the door for counter terms and eventual compromise. To Burgoyne's astonishment Gates finally accepted the British proposals with relatively little argument or change. Under the agreements of the Saratoga Treaty, 6,000 men in the English army stacked their weapons in heaps by the river and marched "with the Honors of War" for Boston. The smashing American victory at Bemis Heights finally secured the upper Hudson Valley and lifted the fatigued spirits of rebels throughout the colonies.

Meanwhile, on the day before Simon Fraser's death, General Clinton had executed a military thrust into the steep, rock-rugged, and beautiful Highlands. American forts Montgomery and Clinton were caught below full strength. A mid-September call for reinforcements up and down the river had produced a discouraging number of militiamen. The garrisons at Verplanck's Point and Stony Point had fallen one after the other, and Clinton's men had crossed the Dunderberg to attack the Poplopen forts from behind. Meanwhile His Majesty's ships *Preston, Dependence, Mercury, Tartar, Diligent, Spitfire, Hotham,* and *Crane,* accompanied by transports, had come about at the mouth of the creek with support forces for the attack. The English fleet cut through the chain across the river on October 6, 1777, and landed unopposed at Fort Constitution. General Putnam's order for the two American frigates to drive down and defend the chain had been a mistake. Both the *Montgomery* and the *Congress* were inexpertly handled and had to be fired to avoid British capture. The English fleet, commanded by Sir James Wallace, continued upriver, burning houses, mills, and any usable vessels they could find. In addition to landing parties, which were sent ashore to destroy certain military targets, land forces were detached by Clinton in the days following his first attacks, with orders to burn whatever rebel stores they found. Major Tryon marched north and destroyed the 1,500-man barracks in "the rebel settlement called the Continental Village." This was an important loss to the Americans, for the barracks magazine was the only one in the Highlands from which rebel troops could draw their new supplies.

The Continental Army had dealt Burgoyne a severe blow at Saratoga, but the Highlands were securely under British control. Clinton did not, however, press his advantage and move immediately on Albany. Finally, after ten days of reconnoitering the river above

General Horatio Gates accepts John Burgoyne's war sword at Saratoga. (*Glens Falls Insurance Company, Glens Falls, New York*)

Newburgh, a combined British fleet and army detachment sailed north to Kingston and anchored in the mouth of the Rondout Creek. There, where Dutchmen had lived since 1615, the galley *Dependence* stood offshore with her sister ships and pounded rebel batteries with cannon fire in preparation for a land assault.

On October 17, 1777, General John Burgoyne surrendered to Horatio Gates at Saratoga—while English General John Vaughan destroyed the village of Kingston. His action was quite unnecessary, possibly cowardly, and at the very least extremely unpopular. The British did not surprise the people in Kingston (it is difficult for a convoy of about thirty vessels to move upriver unnoticed). As the fleet approached Kingston, members of the state legislature, which was in session there, evacuated the town along with practically all its citizens. A handful of militiamen parried with Vaughan as he burned houses and sloops on the Rondout, but the English soon overwhelmed and dispersed this tiny force. By early evening only the stone foundations were left in the main section of the village on a plain above the Creek. American General George Clinton met many of the fleeing villagers on the road to Hurley, but like General Israel Putnam on the opposite side of the river, he arrived too late to avert the conflagration. Vaughan justified what was generally regarded as a senseless act with the offhand comment that all rebel villains in the river valley had been weaned in Kingston and that the town therefore deserved to be destroyed. Even members of the British General Staff could not accept this excuse and pitied Vaughan for his stupidity and arrogance. For the next few days the naval forces under Wallace supported landings on the Hudson's east shore, as storehouses and other buildings in the Tivoli-Rhinebeck region, including the Livingston mansion, were destroyed by fire.

On October 23 the convoy returned through the narrows at Crum Elbow and proceeded back to the Highlands. After the rebuilding of the Dutch church in Kingston a bell was found to replace the one lost in the fire. It was a ship's bell with an adequate tone, but its ring was too familiar and reminded everyone of the *Dependence*, the *Diligent*, and the *Spitfire;* so the congregation had to find a new bell.

The landscape was in the full brilliance of late October when news of the British defeat at Saratoga reached Clinton in the Highlands. The plan for conducting the war from Canada had failed. Clinton had succeeded in gaining control of tidewater Hudson as far north as Clermont in Columbia County, but his lines of communication had not reached Burgoyne, and each was unaware of the other's situation until it was too late for any kind of action. After less than a month's occupation of the Hudson valley, the English fleet sailed slowly back down the river, draining foreign troops from the captured forts like water ebbing from a basin. All the English left behind was the American determination never to lose the Highlands again.

American commanders were quick to admit after Clinton's departure that defensive positions in the Highlands must be concentrated at West Point. In December 1777 General Putnam strongly recommended to General Washington that Fort Constitution be abandoned in favor of a well-placed fortress on the high ground to the west. A month later the Hudson ice at Fort Constitution was thick enough to support General Samuel Parson's brigade as it crossed the river and climbed the hill to spend as severe a period of misery and pain as was ever known at Valley Forge or anywhere else. There was no provision for shelter, and only crude shrub huts could be thrown up in defense from the weather. Kosciuszko arrived from Saratoga in the spring and spent the next two years planning and supervising the construction of the mountain fortress. (It was in 1778 that the famous "great chain" was forged at the Sterling Iron Works, behind West Point; it was stretched across the Hudson at Fort Constitution each spring until the end of the war.)

West Point became about the most important post in America during the last years of the Revolution. Washington moved the main body of his troops there in 1779 after General Anthony ("Mad Anthony") Wayne had recaptured Stony Point and its stores in a heroic midnight bayonet raid. With Washington at West Point, the Hudson valley became a center of national and international affairs. The military location was ideal for any future combat, once the Highlands had been well fortified and the great supply lines through the Fishkill plains were reopened to New England, from which troops, stores, and information were dispatched. The arms captured at Saratoga and Stony Point were brought to West Point, and, as New

York City was in uncontested British control, the upper Hudson assumed the greatest strategic importance.

Then came treason! No one could believe the first reports that West Point had nearly been lost to the English, but the rumors were soon confirmed: Benedict Arnold, the courageous leader of men at Quebec, the hero who was almost killed in a Saratoga redoubt, had conspired against his own country. His cold-blooded conspiracy was uncharacteristic of this war hero, who performed best in the heat of passionate action. The chain of falling dominoes that Arnold had hoped to trigger with the loss of West Point was too dependent on secret meetings and nervous foreign contacts. Major John André was captured with Arnold's information on the defenses of continental fortresses. When news of André's capture reached the Beverly Robinson house, Arnold, his wife, and two of Washington's aides were waiting breakfast for the General's arrival. Arnold read the signals correctly and, seizing the moment, escaped. The soldiers in the household believed that he had been called across the river to West Point on urgent matters, and it was not until his boatmen reached Verplanck's Point, where *H.M.S. Vulture* rode at anchor, that the full impact of Arnold's action was realized. After Major André was summarily hanged in Tappan some believed that the occupation force in Manhattan had been partially repaid for the execution of Nathan Hale. The treason episode was over, except for slight tremors of suspicion that rippled through the Continental Army and were forgotten. Benedict Arnold, once a proud officer for rebel America, had defected. But West Point was secure.

There were, of course, other battles fought on the Hudson—at forts Washington and Lee—as well as a naval skirmish on the Tappan Zee. The Battle of Long Island, Washington's withdrawal from Brooklyn Heights to Manhattan, and the Battle of White Plains were important for American victory, but after Saratoga much of the country's defensive strength was invested on the Hudson at West Point. The English had blundered badly when Howe went to Philadelphia instead of driving toward Albany as he should have done according to Burgoyne's plan. But Washington could not expect the British to ignore the Hudson again, and he therefore ordered the complete fortification of the west hill above Fort Constitution. Ever since those bitter January days in 1778, when General Parsons' troops began the job of digging in, West Point has remained a United States military reservation.

By the end of the war Washington had moved his army to encampments at New Windsor and had established his headquarters at Jonathan Hasbrouck's house in nearby Newburgh. Across from Newburgh the quartermaster-commissary units for the Continental Army's Northern Department lay on the King's Highway just south of the present village of Fishkill. There were hospitals, workshops, magazines, and barracks there in 1779, and more Revolutionary soldiers are buried in the fields at Fishkill than in any other part of the United States.

One of the most famous patriotic newspapers, the *New York Packet,* was printed at Loudon's Press in Fishkill while down the road in John Bailey's shop George Washington's war sword was forged. The intersection of Route 52 and U.S. Route 9 now separates two of the oldest standing buildings in New York State: Trinity Church, which was also used as a hospital, and the Dutch church, where double agent Enoch Crosby was confined.

Henry Knox, whose siege cannon from Ticonderoga had driven the British out of Boston in 1776, also came to Fishkill often during the war, to coordinate supply and training operations. Knox, a six-foot-three-inch, 280-pound hulk of a man, ex-bookstore owner, and artillery expert, also acted as American liaison officer with French military personnel when France finally allied herself with the Revolutionary cause. As General Knox he sat on the military board that sentenced Major André to hang; he commanded West Point from 1781 to 1783, then succeeded Washington as Commander in Chief of the U.S. Army until 1784. He became Washington's Secretary of War in 1787 and retired from public life in 1794. Before leaving the Philadelphia scene, Knox won 1,000 acres of Kentucky land in a lottery, but he never claimed the tract; it has since become synonymous with impregnability and gold, the site of Fort Knox. Knox and his 250-pound wife Lucy then moved to Maine, built a large estate, and lived lavishly. The General died accidentally in 1806 when a chicken bone lodged in his throat, but he had had the pleasure of seeing his first public recommendation materialize when the United States Military Academy was established at West Point in 1802.

Knox was also the driving force behind the formation of the unusual veteran officers' club, the Order of the Cincinnati. One of his great problems as commander at West Point had been pay for his men. He therefore proposed, at Fishkill's Verplanck House, that a society be established as a morale booster for officers with three or more years of service. It would devote itself to patriotic, financial, and fraternal activities aimed at preserving the camaraderie that had prompted the emotional scene at Washington's farewell to his officers at Fraunces Tavern in Manhattan, at which many had been overcome with tears.

The society was named for Lucius Quinctius Cincinnatus, a courageous farmer who had led his fellow Romans against an invading army around the fifth century B.C. Cincinnatus then surprised every one by refusing the reward of a civil office and returning to his wife and farm, thus setting an example for future reserve soldiers. The original member officers of the order included Washington, its first president; Baron Friedrich von Steuben, James Monroe, Kosciuszko, Wayne, John Paul Jones, "Light-Horse Harry" Lee, Knox, and about 4,000 other veterans of the Revolution. Authorship of the motto, *Omnia relinquit servare rempublicam,* which means, "he put aside all to save the nation," has never been established. Major Pierre Charles L'Enfant designed the society's certificate of membership and badge, on which an erroneous additional "n" in the second word has been retained, in honor of tradition, rather than accuracy. The society caused a jealous squabble in New England, where it was accused of trying to create a new aristocracy in the years immediately following the Revolution. Benjamin Franklin shrugged off the crisis—and the Order—as a small matter arising from the small pleasure men get from wearing ribbons in their buttonholes. Today many state chapters are practically inactive. Among honorary members of the society have been King Gustavus VI of Sweden; Presidents Andrew Jackson, Zachary Taylor, Franklin Pierce, James Buchanan, Ulysses S. Grant, Grover Cleveland, Benjamin Harrison, William McKinley, Theodore and Franklin Roosevelt, William Howard Taft, Woodrow Wilson, Warren Harding, Herbert Hoover, and Harry Truman; and Generals Omar Bradley, Mark Clark, and Matthew Ridgeway. In a 1952 Washington ceremony Winston Churchill received his badge and certification as a descendant of

Reuben Murray, his great-great-great-grandfather, who had served in the Revolution and had been a member of the Connecticut chapter of the order. "It is a most memorable event in my crowded life," Churchill said. "I am in the interesting situation of having fought on both sides of the war between us and we."

After the signing of the peace in Paris on September 3, 1783, the Hudson became quiet again. General Washington met Sir Guy Carleton in the Livingston House at Dobbs Ferry and concluded arrangements for evacuating English troops from New York City. It was time to celebrate, and before all the English soldiers had been loaded onto transports in Upper Bay, the American army behind Knox was marching into Manhattan—this time in triumph.

Once the English had left New York, Hudson's valley came alive with postwar activity. Expansion west through the Mohawk valley and talk of linking New York with the Great Lakes generated interest among tidewater manufacturers, but politicians were decidedly less enthusiastic about the costs of such a venture. Farming counties in the valley prospered and villages boomed with industry engendered by the river. Sloop captains shipped farm produce to New York and brought manufactured goods to upriver towns. There was growth throughout the river region, and families established themselves on the land. Life was becoming more than a matter of mere survival, and men began to build promising futures.

When the United States went to war with England again in 1812, many landowners who had prospered in the Hudson River valley since the Revolution were reluctant to give full support to their country in its challenge of the greatest sea power in the world. New York shipbuilders were delighted, however, as were many seamen who had been without profitable occupation for years. In the first six months of the war twenty-six privateers were built and fitted out in East and North River yards. The *General Armstrong*, built by Adam and Noah Brown at their Houston Street yard, was the largest ship to come off East River ways during the war. Not far from Wall Street privateers were also built in Harry Eckford's and Christian Bergh's shipyards, both located on the East River near Gouverneur's slip.

American shipping was severely hampered, however, by the British men-of-war, which effectively blockaded New York harbor. Sandy

Hook pilots did their best to run ships through the blockade, but most privateers and even some frigates were forced to exit through the hazardous Hell Gate channel into Long Island Sound. The immediate problem for shippers were the men-of-war below the Narrows, but New York City also faced the threat of possible naval attack. To meet the crisis of an inadequately defended harbor, orders were given to build fortifications on several North River islands. A star fort was designed and constructed on Liberty Island, and a circular battery with heavy gun emplacements was completed on Ellis Island, to defend the city against a combined land and sea expeditionary force that never attacked. Shore batteries, arsenals, and earthworks were expanded and improved on Lower Manhattan, at Governors Island, and at Fort Lafayette; Fort Richmond commanded the Narrows from high ground on Staten Island. Much of the labor that went into building these fortifications was voluntary, as it had been during the Revolution, and craftsmen responded in organized bodies to the call for construction aid.

Resolutions were also adopted authorizing recruitment of militia companies in New York City and enlistment offices were opened to any and all city or upstate volunteers. The city's artillery and infantry were consolidated and mustered into service under well-trained officers. The war was generally unpopular in Hudson River counties, but reserve forces were reactivated in towns all along the river and transported by sloop to New York City to reinforce the garrisons there. At the end of the city's general mobilization period, there were move than 20,000 men under arms, all volunteers with the exception of 1,000 United States regulars. Fortunately, however, the war ended before a strong attack could be mounted; nevertheless the city and its harbor were well fortified against any new threats from the sea.

During the War of 1812, after American victories on the Niagara frontier were repeated in New Orleans, Britain finally realized the strength of United States arms and reluctantly acknowledged that reconquest of the "colonies" would be futile. Twenty days after the signing of the peace with England, New Yorkers heard the news and celebrated with public dinners and parades. Officially the two countries returned to the prewar status quo. The United States had yielded nothing and remained resolute in asserting its own sovereignty. The blockade was lifted from Lower Bay and a new age of steam took command of the Hudson.

In 1817 the West Point foundry kindled its forges behind Constitution Island and contracted to manufacture and supply heavy ordnance for the U.S. Army. The foundry's manager Robert Parrott developed the famous smooth-action "Parrott gun," which became a prominent weapon in the Civil War. Iron ore was unloaded from sloops and canal boats at the foundry docks to be pounded and bored into artillery pieces for the Union Army. Many Hudson River men followed these guns into the South and helped to swell New York State contingents fighting under Grant to nearly half a million men. There were North River seamen on the *Monitor* when it sailed south from Brooklyn to meet the *Merrimac* in the historic battle of the ironclads. Another "filthy ironpot," the *Manhattan,* was launched from a Jersey City shipyard in 1864 and sailed in Admiral David Glasgow Farragut's fleet toward the Gulf of Mexico for the Battle of Mobile Bay. New York and New Jersey yards built and fitted warships of both traditional and modern iron design to aid in the blockade of the South. The northern war machine had been tooled up, and the major Hudson River ports were busy in all areas of construction and transportation.

New York State contributed heavily, both in wealth and manpower, to the Union cause. The state provided the greatest number of soldiers—50,000—the most money, and the largest quantity of supplies for the Union Army. But when the war was over the cities and villages of New York, like similar towns all over the country, were faced with the problem of returning soldiers—and, of course, with the problem of soldiers who did not return.

A flood of foreign immigrants to New York City ameliorated the loss of craftsmen and tradesmen during the war, but the rural areas were hard hit. Farming regions in the Hudson and Mohawk valleys had lost their young men. Their sons had been drafted from the harvests and were forever lost somewhere in Alabama, Virginia or maybe Tennessee. Emigrants from upstate farming regions also crowded the cities, providing labor for the factories but increasing the losses to small rural communities. Negro troops returned to every city on the tidewater Hudson, but not every city was happy to have them back. Employment was a problem, and most black veterans were forced to take laboring jobs or no jobs at all. Lives were suddenly rearranged by economic necessities, and those who could not adjust to the postwar mood were the living casualties of the struggle. High employment for some classes cut down on the relief rolls, and the generosity of organizations all over the state provided care for wounded veterans and needy dependents. But spiraling inflation and pockets of prosperity widened the gap between rich and poor. Industry expanded along the Hudson waterfront, and the surge in commercial transportation on the river was unparalleled. Corrupt politicians corrupted military contractors or vice versa and kickbacks from the sale of war materials made more than a few men incredibly wealthy. The war had torn apart institutions and shattered families, but it had officially at least, unified the country, and the future was to be based on growth and healing. People looked ahead and tried to leave memories of the secession behind.

In the days immediately following the end of the war, however, there was a single great outpouring of grief across the country. President Abraham Lincoln was shot and Hudson's valley mourned as his funeral train slowly retraced the route he had so triumphantly taken from Springfield for his inauguration.

Not since General Lafayette's nostalgic hero's return to the Revolutionary battlefields in 1824 had so many people come to the river to pay homage to a great man. Some had gone to watch when Lincoln had first traveled across New York State and down the Hudson's eastern shore, on his way to his inauguration, but in those early years he had not yet inspired the esteem, sympathy, and love that thousands of people now waited along the roadbed to express.

When Lincoln's train reached the river in New Jersey it was lightered across the Hudson to the Chambers Street passenger station in Manhattan and eventually drawn uptown to the station at Thirtieth Street. Locomotives were burning coal by then, and the Hudson River Railroad maintained continuity on its section of the run by supplying the same two engines that had drawn the inaugural special. The Constitution acted as pilot locomotive, while the Union followed ten minutes later with what many called the "ghost train."

The fact that the Union drew the cars while the Constitution guided the way was not lost on any of the people gathered to watch them pass.

Five days after leaving Washington, the train, carrying dignitaries and members of Lincoln's family, started up the Hudson. All along the route steamboats saluted with flags at half-staff, and reports from tiny cannons boomed across the water. Stores closed in cities and hamlets all along the right of way, and civic and religious groups lined the tracks to pay their respects. Fraternal and military organizations provided bands, while uniformed members of these groups stood at attention as the painfully slow-moving locomotives passed in muffled silence. Dirges were played, and ministers read from the Bible, but plain citizens simply watched the train move north. People lined the banks of both shores of the river, and boats of every description nosed their bows against the rocks a few feet from the tracks. Most towns along the route prepared shrines or archways and draped them with the colors of mourning. Some carried mottoes like the one at Hastings-on-Hudson: "We will cherish the memory of Abraham Lincoln by supporting the principles of free government for which he suffered martyrdom."

At Tarrytown, under the inscription "Bear him gently to rest," an American flag was also painted on the side of a building. Across from Fort Montgomery, where the tiny grade crossing of Manitou is today, a minister and his congregation knelt in the cinders for hours until the train finally passed by. A few miles farther north, a thousand cadets and regulars from West Point held a brief ceremony as field pieces echoed in the Highlands.

It was dark when the train stopped in Poughkeepsie and the passengers disembarked for a light supper. Matthew Vassar placed magnolia branches by the casket, and a band played funeral processionals. Finally the train reached East Albany, where the casket was removed, placed on a gun carriage, and ferried across the river. The streets in the state capital were awash with light from torches and flaming tar barrels. Lincoln had addressed a joint session of the state legislature during his last visit to Albany, and now his body was placed on a simple bier before the speaker's stand. At the end of the ceremonies for the dead President, Thurlow Weed's daughter draped the casket with an American flag, and on the following day President Lincoln was taken west on the New York Central.

One of the most interesting inventions ever to be launched in New York waters was John Holland's submarine. In May 1897 the *Holland,* appropriately nicknamed "Holland's cigar," slid into the water and, according to a *New York Times* reporter, "floated trim and true to her estimated water line." The *Holland* subsequently became the first submarine ever accepted by the U.S. Navy, and its inventor, who was born in Ireland's Shannon River valley, has justifiably been called "the father of the modern submarine." His basic design and operating principles have been adopted and advanced in German, Russian, English, Japanese, and, of course, American submarines.

Robert Fulton had developed a successful plunging boat and torpedo device, which even interested Napoleon for a time, but both inventions were ultimately abandoned by the French. Fulton also demonstrated his submarine for the British Admiralty and was offered compensation for his craft on the grounds that the introduction of this kind of "awful war machine" would put England on a par with other navies. Even earlier, David Bushnell's hand-operated *Turtle* had almost sunk a British warship during the Revolution. The *Turtle* approached an English frigate anchored in New York harbor and submerged practically alongside the ship. Bushnell had devised a method for attaching explosives to a wooden ship by inserting them in a boring tool, which was then dug into the hull. But at this first attempt, the device would not penetrate the wood, and the *Turtle* eventually lost contact with the frigate altogether.

John Holland's first submarine had been launched in 1878 and called, appropriately enough, "Boat No. 1." It was a fourteen-foot, one-man vessel and had been financed by the Fenian Society. These radical Irishmen had become interested in Holland's work and were excited by the possibilities of a submarine that could be carried in a conventional vessel transported about, and lowered through the bottom of the ship for purposes of attack. They also financed a second Holland submarine, which a member of the working press dubbed the *Fenian Ram.* This new plunging boat was given sea trials in New York harbor and successfully passed back and forth under steamboats and barges. The vessel was equipped with a gasoline engine for running on the surface and an air tube for firing torpedos; the latter had been designed by John Ericson, the shipbuilder who had launched the *Monitor*. But the Fenians became disenchanted with Holland's handling of the *Ram* project and pirated the vessel from its berth in Jersey City. They took the submarine to New Haven, where, after several attempts to operate it failed, they eventually discarded it behind an old brass works.

In 1886 Holland began to build his third submarine at Fort Lafayette, but this project ended in disaster when the ways collapsed before it was launched. Further development of the submarine was then delayed at least ten years while Holland sought financial backing for another ship. Eventually, this small, candid, resilient Irishman built his successful submarine, and after years of frustration and red tape the U.S. Navy finally commissioned it in 1900. The *Holland* actually served, however, only in an obscure capacity as a training vessel. In a few years it was retired, sold, and put on exhibition in a Bronx park. It was later sold for scrap, and in 1914 Holland himself died in obscurity one month before a German U-boat sank three British ships.

At about the same time that Holland had been trying to sell navy officials on the idea of submarine warfare, naval intelligence was considering conclusive reports that its munitions works at Fort Lafayette in New York harbor were no longer safe from long-range guns. In March 1899 Congress appropriated $600,000 for the purchase of land and erection of buildings on an island in the Hudson which would be known as the U.S. Naval Ammunition Depot, Iona Island, New York. No one is sure how the island, located on the Race and practically touching Bear Mountain State Park, received its original name but fifty years before its sale to the navy, C. W. Grant, M.D., was raising grapes there and cultivating 2,000 to 3,000 fruit trees. Subsequently a hotel and other "country facilities" were built there, and prizefighter John L. Sullivan trained on the island. Iona Island was also a popular destination for holiday excursions and picnics. One old river man recalled that the Knights of Columbus occasionally ran a barge party up to Iona, and on one excursion, he said, a black-stacked tug had spent more time tied alongside the barge for refreshment than it did up front towing. But the most fanciful tale told in the area alleges that one night, when a conductor on the West Shore Railroad called out the station stop, "Iona Island," a rough individual stood up toe to toe with the trainman and growled, "Hell, I own a farm, but I ain't braggin' about it."

As a naval depot, Iona was the second leg of an important ammunition-supply triangle. Shells and artillery canisters for naval guns were shipped to Iona from the Lake Denmark bulk-storage plant in Dover, New Jersey (Picatinny Arsenal). At Iona they were assembled and shipped to the issuing station at Fort Lafayette. This production triangle was responsible for supplying ammunition to much of the Atlantic fleet during both world wars. Production was eventually suspended, however, and in 1967 Iona Island became part of the New York State park system.

Around the Dunderberg from Iona Island, anchored in Seylmaker's Reach adjacent to Tomkins Cove, is part of the National Defense Reserve fleet. Commonly called "liberty ships" and numbering in the hundreds, these vessels are controlled by the Maritime Administration of the United States Department of Commerce. The defense fleet was created by Congress in 1946 in the event of a national emergency that would require a steady reserve of cargo ships. Some of the ships are of World War I vintage, and many have been redeployed since World War II to transport Marshall Plan material to Europe and to supply allied forces in Suez, Korea, and Vietnam. The ships are continuously overhauled to preserve their machinery and to guard against the corrosive effects of the river and the weather.

When the United States finally came out of isolation and entered World War I, New York State was again called upon to furnish a great proportion of the men, money, and materials necessary for such a global conflict. New York harbor became a great naval base and shipyard; warships passed continually through the Narrows. New York was also one of the most important ports of embarkation for soldiers ordered overseas. The Watervliet Arsenal produced cannon and various other types of artillery; smaller companies subcontracted to manufacture vast numbers of defense items, including electronic equipment, gun sights, and clothing. Again half a million men left

"Liberty ships" anchored near the shad grounds of Peekskill Bay

The Hudson's channel, left of these silhouettes

New York to fight, and of this total 190,000 were from the sixteen Hudson River counties; the largest percentage came from the greater New York City area. To augment naval-construction activity in New Jersey, Manhattan, and Brooklyn, the Marvel Shipyard in Newburgh shifted to defense contracts, and several transports sailed for France from this upriver town.

New York's Catskill water-supply system was opened in 1917, and guarded all along its route to prevent sabotage. The Poughkeepsie Railroad Bridge was also guarded by armed soldiers, some of whom were fed holiday dinners through chain-link fences by girls whom they later returned to marry. The bridge carried troops and material toward Boston, while beneath its span the New York Central hauled freight down both sides of the Hudson. After the Armistice, the river was jammed with troop ships returning home; among them was *Leviathan,* a hulking German ship caught in the Port of New York at the outbreak of hostilities and refitted for transport duty, in spite of the crew's attempt to totally destroy its machinery. Most of the men came home, but in another twenty years Hudson River towns were ready to repeat the process all over again. Men who as schoolboys had been trained in civilian defense during World War I were called twenty years later to fight in France, Italy, Germany, and the Pacific. World War II challenged, and there was a concerted effort in the Hudson River valley to supply its quota of everything required to win. West Point provided engineers and officers, as it had done since the Revolution. The Marvel Shipyard built floating drydocks, and the arsenals at Watervliet and the Iona Island triangle continued to turn out weaponry. The iron and steel mills in the Tri-Cities forged ore from the Adirondacks into heavy machinery and other vital war material. Grain from Albany elevators was shipped downriver for destinations around the world, even at the expense of New York farmers, who faced serious feed shortages. The apparel industry throughout the Hudson Valley doubled its output of uniforms, heavy clothing, and boots for all theaters of battle. New York sent more than a half-million men to this war, and determined, imaginative women mastered skills necessary for filling vacancies in defense plants. Scows and tugboats were built in river towns to cope with increased shipments of goods earmarked for the New York City

naval stations and distribution abroad. Factories were again converted into defense plants, and many new installations were constructed. The demands of large military convoys—sometimes including from twenty to fifty ships—put a tremendous burden on the
limited number of Sandy Hook pilots, who would climb down from
one boat in Lower Bay to race back up the harbor and guide
another.

When the war ended, men came back to the Hudson on the big
liners, passed the Statue of Liberty lighted in the harbor, and were
smothered in emotion on North River piers. Before very long, however, New Yorkers were called to fight in Korea under the banner
of the United Nations, and the defense plants were retooled all over
again. Cynics point to the war cycle as the inevitable imbalance of
an ambitious ideology, but men die for men not ideals, and the
hardship and grief of all our armed conflicts have been sustained
by ordinary people in the Hudson valley, as in all areas of the nation.

FIVE

FOR THE first fifty years of this century the biggest event on the Hudson River each June was the Intercollegiate Rowing Association Regatta at Poughkeepsie. The importance and fame of the race extended far beyond mere university rivalries, and Boat Race Day was a major social, as well as sporting, event. University eights from a dozen or more colleges competed for the four-mile prize in a punishing test of skill, strength, and will.

The Poughkeepsie course was about the best straight four-mile stretch of water available in the country, and it was more than wide enough to accommodate several shells abreast, as well as a variety of spectator boats. All river traffic was suspended before the races, and the U.S. Coast Guard tried to control the flotilla of spectator boats clustered near the finish line. For years an observation train was operated along the west shore and provided the best continuing view of the race only yards away. A cannon on the railroad bridge signaled the winning lane, after which the school's colors were lowered from there for further identification.

It is difficult to estimate how many people came to the river on Boat Race Day. They arrived by just about every possible kind of transportation and crowded into boats of every description. The navy usually sent a small fleet, and Day liners were thrown off even keels as thousands of passengers jammed the deck railings to see the final sprints. Vincent Astor's *Normourhal* was a prominent fixture near the finish line, and before the race the ferry made countless trips to the west shore, where people climbed the rocks for a better view.

Eugene O'Neill spent a strange interlude on the fantail of a yacht during one race, while spectators overhead on the railroad bridge had the best view of the whole river and hoped that no train would come across in the meantime. The observation train was a rolling grandstand of about sixty canvas-covered flatcars powered by a steam locomotive at each end. The best seats were near the officials' and press car in the middle of the train, which was generally kept abreast of the crews during most of the race; engineers at the head of the train were sometimes known to speed up to give their friends in the rear engine a better-than-average view of the shells.

There were three races on the program: freshman eights for two miles, junior-varsity eights for three miles, and varsity eights for four miles. Between eighteen and twenty minutes was the average time for the four miles, and any attempt to break the course record depended on favorable wind and tides. Columbia College won the first I.R.A. regatta in 1895 in 21 minutes and 25 seconds. A year later the Big Red crew from Cornell slashed this time to 19 minutes and 59 seconds. But the record time for the varsity distance was a blistering 18 minutes and 12 3/5 seconds set by the University of California in 1939. The 1922 Navy crew was clocked at 13 minutes and 33 3/5 seconds for the junior-varsity record.

Although all the events on Boat Race day were held between 3:00 and 7:00 P.M. on one Saturday afternoon, out-of-town spectators checked into local hotels days in advance to watch the oarsmen, who had been training on the Hudson for weeks. Most major newspapers sent reporters to grind out thousands of words on the regatta, and over the years reputations were made on the consistency of predictions. English bookmakers posted odds on the varsity eights, and local sportsmen took money from anyone with a mind to wager.

The shell houses were all within one or two miles of one another along both shores. The crews were quartered all over town, even in Vassar College dormitories. Regulations for competitors were so strict in those days that one Cornell oarsman was not allowed to visit or even to speak to his fiancée, who happened to live in Poughkeepsie. On one June afternoon the air over the Hudson turned blue when the Syracuse coach took a walk after lunch and found his boys playing softball with a group of Marist brothers. Alumni and fraternity groups stole one another's mascots or painted giant school letters on shale slabs along the west shore. The block letters that Cornell, Princeton, Columbia, Navy, and other schools repainted for years have now faded or disappeared altogether.

One of the most important men to attend the races year after year was George ("Building Boats to Build Men") Pocock, the Seattle craftsman in whose shells most of the crews competed. Pocock was on hand to take orders every summer and designed each new shell to be hand-built especially for the Hudson River.

When all the prerace hoopla surrounding the I.R.A. was reduced by the automobile to only a few hours, the regatta at Poughkeepsie lost much of its appeal. Hotels were half empty, merchants complained that their cash drawers were the same, and fewer rowing patrons sat under the slowly revolving black-iron fans of Smith Brothers Restaurant. Smith Brothers, the Day Line, and Boat Race day had been synonymous with Poughkeepsie in the minds of thousands of people who had made all three an annual June event. By the mid-1940s, however, most of the old sheen had tarnished. The observation train was dismantled in World War II and never rebuilt. In the late 1940s the race committee cut the varsity distance to three miles after debating the notion that the extra mile was too strenuous for young oarsmen. And when the city refused budget appropriations for much needed visitor and boathouse facilities, the Association accepted an invitation to hold the regatta in Marietta, Ohio; after a year or two it was transferred to Syracuse, New York, where it is still run each June. When the colleges vacated their Hudson boathouses they left usable equipment behind so that local high schools could begin their own rowing programs. The 1950s were growing years for those schools, and by the mid-1960s as many as twelve or fifteen shells would be on the water on a given afternoon. Crewing has become very popular on the secondary-school level and as a club sport in many colleges as well.

Before and just after the Civil War, there had been no distinction between professional and amateur oarsmen. No committees determined who was and who was not eligible to win the substantial prize money offered in those days. Newburgh's most famous oarsmen, the Ward brothers, won their first important race on their home waters in 1857. The Wards were all sloop captains who worked the brick runs from Coeymens to Manhattan's Fifty-Second Street. They rowed hard in their spare time, however, and became the best-known oarsmen of their day. Josh Ward went on to capture the single-scull championship and was well paid for his art. Mothers named their boys after him, and Thomas Eakins painted his portrait, but Josh eventually returned to the sloop business.

The first pair of spoon oars were made in Poughkeepsie by George Polk, and it was there that the American championships were held on July 18, 1865. Boats were named in the early years and were often much better known than the men who rowed them. Prize money for the championship was $6,000. Ten thousand people poured into Poughkeepsie and wagered as much as $100,000 on the results of the race. The distance was five miles rowed, two and a half miles each way. It turned out to be a dual meet between the Biglin brothers, of Newburgh, and the *Stranger* crew from Poughkeepsie.

Conditions were not ideal on race day, and the heavy boats plowed ponderously through the whitecaps. The New York crew took an early lead and was ahead as it rounded the stake boat, but the *Stranger* began to close the distance in the final mile. In the last half-mile, as the noise from the enormous crowd began to wash over the oarsmen, the Biglin brothers steered their boat to cut off the *Stranger* and win the race.

The Poughkeepsie boat and its backers naturally claimed a foul. To the accompaniment of all the shoving and shouting that characterize this kind of incident the *Stranger* crew complained to referee Charles Gausman, who was then driven with the other judges directly to the Poughkeepsie Hotel. There they attempted to conduct a closed meeting.

But crowds of thugs and roughnecks kicked in the door and

crawled in through the windows. There were so many people jammed into the small room that a weak man would have suffocated. One reporter wrote that there was "as murderous a set of villains as the eye ever gazed upon who began at once to intimidate the referee with drawn pistols, knives, and clubs." Nationally known prizefighter Joe Coburn had bet heavily on the *Stranger* crew and promised to "lick anyone in the room single-handed," but his challenge was met with cries of "shoot him," "grab the money," and "burn the hotel."

The room finally quieted enough for Gausman to announce that the Biglins had won the championship in thirty-seven minutes and twenty seconds; he barely escaped with his life. The next day in a downtown saloon Stevens, the *Stranger*'s bowman, knocked down and killed a man who had accused him of selling the race. In those days the violence after such events was so widespread that a lady never went into the streets of Poughkeepsie on a race or election night.

It is April when high-school oarsmen go down to the Hudson to exhaust themselves against the tides. Spring brings people back onto the outside decks of the Staten Island ferry, and shad run to spawn in the upriver flats of their birth. The Hudson's water is cold and high and mud-colored from the mountain streams. On spring's first warm day, a schoolboy running in the shadow of a river house kicks a sock and finds it frozen in the frost, but the boardwalk at Coney Island comes alive again, and the boarded-up windows of Adirondack lodges are reopened. The warm season comes a month later there, but the snow does melt, and spring pools appear in every crimp and fold in the land.

Very late spring is also the white-water racing season on the upper Hudson at North Creek. There, politicians and local woodsmen compete in the Adirondacks' annual kayak regatta. The course is from North Creek a few miles down the Hudson to Riparius. The river is rugged in this upper section, and constant dunkings in freezing water force many men out of the race before they even near the finish line.

Although a cold Hudson River bath may appeal to only a handful of people, thousands of others are attracted by the mineral waters

The Performing Arts Center at Saratoga Springs

and natural elixirs of the Saratoga spas. A certain primitive charm, as well as the healthy effects of the spas, brings thousands of enthusiasts back again and again. Washing through the ground deep beneath the earth's surface, glacial rivers absorb and interact with minerals from the rocks until the natural gas produced by this process forces the water to the surface, where the state bottles it for sale. Indians came to the spas sporadically to renew their courage, and it was they who introduced white trappers to the beauties of the strange water. August is Saratoga's month, and people come from great distances to see the horses run, watch the New York City Ballet, hear Van Cliburn play Tchaikovsky with the Philadelphia Orchestra, or immerse themselves in mineral waters trapped underground for 10,000 years.

In August the Hudson in this region is gentle, as is suggested by the town of Stillwater. But in the tidewater belt sudden summer showers and long-brewing storms whip the Hudson into frenzies that are the undoing of many boatmen. Without such storms, however, corn fields crack dry, and the smell and taste of automobile metal seems to linger in the air of steaming cities.

It is the time of year for Washington Irving stories and long afternoon naps. Boat excursions around Manhattan or up the Hudson to West Point offer history, beauty, and entertainment to anyone interested in spending a few hours on the river. People from the Bronx eat cheese on the lawns of the New York Botanical Gardens and listen to the New York Philharmonic play Wagner under stars that turn out to be lights on commercial jets landing at La Guardia Airport. It is easier than ever now for New Yorkers to swim in Lake George or canoe near North Creek, to explore seventeenth-century Dutch buildings at Van Cortlandt's Manor or tour New York City's many museums. Summer is a good time of year just to sit and talk in the shade, have a beer, and watch the river flow by, but it is also the season for discovery.

Of all the homes in the Hudson valley one of the most unusual, certainly, is Olana, the nineteenth-century estate of the late Frederick Church. Church was about the last member of the school of painting deriving its name from the river valley. He designed, built, and furnished his villa in a style that might be described as Moorish-Italianeclectic. The whole house was treated as a work of art. Perched on a hill hard by the Rip Van Winkle Bridge and commanding a view west toward the site where the Mountain House once stood, it represents the varied interests of a man at home with romantic art, Eastern cultures, and precise symmetry. The house is filled with art objects that have their specific places in rooms that combine history, regionalism, and religion, often beautifully. Each aspect of the house reveals a different aspect of Church's life and character.

Light is a dominant theme in Olana. It enters from unexpected locations, so that objects are illuminated perhaps from three rooms away. Statues are reflected in mirrors so that they can be seen from half-a-dozen different locations in as many rooms, each view part of the artist's conscious design. Knights' shields, inlaid fireplace paneling, interior windows, and mirrors beam sunlight into corners to illuminate even the one room that is painted all black. It is difficult to imagine anyone living at Olana. Church even attempted to maintain symmetry by building an artificial lake to balance his view of the Hudson. The house was nearly lost on the auction block in the early 1960s, but a group of interested preservationists rallied support until the state acquired the land for a museum and park. Olana is now not only a fascinating museum but also an active monument to an unusual man.

Not very far south of Olana, near Saugerties, New York, another monument rises on a hillside. It is "Opus 40," a massive piece of environmental sculpture carved out of bluestone by Harvey Fite. He has already been at work on his free-form design for twenty-six years and will spend many more chiseling, chipping, and fitting chunks of rock into a six-acre series of platforms, staircases, pits, and passageways. This work is not meant merely to be looked at; it is intended to stimulate participation with all the senses.

Fite is a teacher and sculptor, and what began as an outdoor gallery for his work has become a gigantic creative masterpiece in itself, not unlike the natural setting for the late David Smith's metal designs in a field near the Lake George village of Bolton Landing. The last quarry master's wife sold Mr. Fite the land, from which rock to pave New York City sidewalks had been dug 100 years before. (One can easily recognize the river's economic, navigational, and cultural

progress here if he digresses long enough to think of earlier days.)
The sculptor, looking very much like a Stone Age warrior returning
home with a skull in each hand, carries smooth rocks to where he
can chip them with special hard-tipped tools before he places them
precisely, in keeping with his concept. "Opus 40" will be completed
only when Harvey Fite feels and knows that it is right. It is not
tack-on art; "it will be integral and whole when it is finished." Bar-
ring human intervention, the massive bluestone design could endure
for 10,000 years and be left standing when other contemporary rock
structures have crashed to earth.

In architecture and sculpture Church and Fite have each exercised
individual freedom, limited only by his own creativity and the
disciplines of his particular art form. Others, like the river drifters,
share the same free spirit but theirs is the less formal art of leisure
and the ability to move on at will.

In a linoleum, tar-paper, plywood, cardboard, and corrugated-
tin shack at the river's edge near Peekskill, two toothless, old-looking
prospectors sit by a primitive stove laughing. They laugh quite a lot
because they are happy. Cash comes from odd jobs, friends, and railroad men, who secretly envy the careless life that these two men
share by the river. There is no authentic furniture in the hut, only
boxes covered with old rugs and discarded remnants. "We've been
all around the country, but for some reason the freights keep bringing us back here."

Except for those rare periods of labor when the men go into town,
life around the hut is leisurely. "When you finish taking a nap in
on the cot you come outside and sleep in the grass. Maybe fish a
little. Sometimes Pete'll come along with a quarta ale and a couple'a
potatoes to bake. Freedom is what we have here. No taxes, no cars,
no strikes, no women, no worries! And by next winter we will have
the chain saw paid off."

Forty miles north of Peekskill John Burroughs catalogued the
same problems but achieved a far less simplistic escape. Burroughs
came to the West Park vicinity of the Hudson below Kingston, and
lived with his family in a house called Riverby. In 1895 he decided
that he needed another place to work besides Riverby and chose a
swampy location a mile or two back from the river, where he built

John Burroughs's Slabsides (*John Mylod*)

a cottage named Slabsides. Friends wondered why he preferred a swamp when the Hudson was so near, but he suggested that occasional glimpses of the river through the trees were more compelling than having the great expanse of the water constantly spread out before him. When he bought the land his wife reminded him that he always had money to spend on his own projects but claimed to be broke when it came to painting the upstairs bedroom or buying draperies for the parlor at Riverby. But the white-bearded Burroughs replied that he did not like paint and went to work at Slabsides. He called it a withdrawal, "the taking up of a new position from which to renew the attack."

Although much is written of Henry David Thoreau's life in the woods, Burroughs knew the Hudson countryside as well as Thoreau knew Walden and was a far better naturalist. He was a friend of presidents and industrialists but remained a man unto himself. Opposite Slabsides on the other side of the Hudson the mammoth Vanderbilt mansion, with its imported rooms, represented a totally different set of values, which Burroughs understood but dismissed in favor of the quiet retreat and celery patch where he could observe and reflect upon nature. He wrote when he wanted to, and Vassar girls on excursions were amused by his talk. Sometimes he walked back and forth to Riverby daily in the winter, stopping at one of the Hudson views, where he might have seen one of James Roosevelt's iceboats skimming across the river at eighty miles an hour, racing a train, or about to tack past a pine-tree turning marker jammed in the ice. At other times he remained at Slabsides for weeks or went with his wife and Walt Whitman to Poughkeepsie to visit Vassar professors. But Burroughs could lure his wife up the hill only twice. She came in the beginning to see the finished house he had built in the forest a short distance from a long rock ledge. A few years later she thought it appropriate to visit Slabsides once again to dine with President and Mrs. Theodore Roosevelt.

John Burroughs' house is just about the same today as it was when he died in 1921 (it is opened once or twice a year for Burroughs Society meetings). Only heavy mesh screening on the windows has been added to this simple two-story cabin. Whereas other late nineteenth-century homes in this region of the valley were constructed along the lines of Vanderbilt's estate, Burroughs' design would have to be called "Hudson River primitive." When the early Dutch settlers first arrived on the Hudson they constructed one-story log or board cabins, each with a small loft. Some had chimneys of mud and wood and later of stone, brick, or both. Thatched roofs were replaced in time by pine shingles. These houses were sufficient for the first years on the land but eventually gave way to larger stone or brick houses. Few, if any, of these temporary homes remain.

Slabsides derives its name from the slab, or first slice cut from a log; the house thus gives a log-cabin effect, but it also has interior walls of wood siding instead of mud-filled chinks. Its furniture is made of saplings, and knotted cedar posts support the porch roof and the porch. Burroughs "quarried" stone from the ridge nearby and fitted the blocks into a chimney forty feet high. The swamp at his doorstep was drained, and men planted celery in long rows toward his fresh-water spring. He wrote at a rough wooden table; his bed was made of birch trees. Up a steep flight of stairs was a guest room with the same kind of first-floor furnishings. Burroughs found peace there; as Thoreau would have said, he "confronted" nature and life. Burroughs did not, however, make an issue of confronting nature. Living, for him, was something one had to do but did not go around bragging about. "Plenty of others are doing the same thing," he said, but none went about it in quite the same way. Paintings and sculpture, which crowded the walls and halls and even the ceilings of the Vanderbilt main house, were absent from Slabsides. The forest was Burroughs' gallery. He would take a maple leaf, bigger than the palm of his hand, hold it to the sun, trace its veins, feel the ribbed texture of the surface as if trying to feel its color through his fingertips. This was his art.

At about the time that Burroughs was still living in Riverby, Joe Jefferson was making a fortune, in fact a career, out of his lead role in Dion Boucicault's play *Rip Van Winkle*. After charming New York City audiences for seasons, Jefferson took the play on the road and toured all the larger towns in the Hudson valley, New England, and old England. Afterward, his son Joseph Jefferson, Jr., played the role for another generation.

In the years after the Civil War, theaters and theater companies emerged in dozens of upstate cities. Yonkers, Tarrytown, Peekskill, Newburgh, Fishkill, Matteawan, Poughkeepsie, Kingston, Hudson, and Albany developed interest in the drama "and other aspects of civilization." They built large opera houses, which catered to theater, music, minstrels, and oratory. They were by no means limited to local talent. New York City companies brought the New York shows and all the popular performers to these towns. Lecture series were begun in most cities. Well-known orators, as well as hacks, toured the circuit. Ralph Waldo Emerson was popular along the Hudson, where he spoke on such "transcendental" topics as how to decorate one's home. Political cartoonist Thomas Nast had $20,000 worth of lectures lined up for one season, and did considerably better than nine-year-old Ralph Bughan, the Boy Orator, whose favorite speech was "The Wreck of the Hesperus."

In addition to offering touring performances, the opera houses were centers of local entertainment. Church choirs, orchestras, bands, and soloists performed everything from Beethoven to "Nearer My God to Thee." Inferior touring companies did, of course, try to foist a certain amount of theatrical claptrap upon a rather discerning clientele, but these houses also offered the best of Shakespeare and Gilbert & Sullivan.

Dion Boucicault put a stop to the "star system" when he pioneered in the use of professional stock companies. Under the old system a well-known performer would travel around the country playing with local theater groups and packing the houses for the amateur companies. There was a good deal of profit in this system for the star, but the rest of the theater suffered. Boucicault's professional players were gathered together by well-known performers, who would then take them on tour. They would stay a week each in the larger cities, usually performing three or four different plays. Plays by such American writers as Clyde Fitch, George Washington Cable, Augustin Daly, William Gillette, and David Belasco were popular in Hudson River towns. Laura Keene, who was playing in *Our American Cousin* when Lincoln was shot, brought her company to Hudson River theaters for many years. Ethel Barrymore, Grace George, Lillian Russell, Jefferson, Boucicault, and Edwin Booth also returned season after season to perform in tidewater communities. Interest in performers was rather widespread and not limited to any one city. Posters were often pasted upside down to attract attention, and it was during this period that the traveling companies first began advertising on the fronts of new buildings. Advance men came to town, and newspapers were glad to publicize events in connection with a "swell" show. Josh Billings, Petroleum Nasby, John Phoenix, Artemus Ward, and other newspaper humorists satirized the cultural rush in the last half of the nineteenth century and played it out in their columns with style, suggesting that anything outside New York City was culturally pretentious.

Stock companies were still operating in the river counties just prior to World War I, but the response had diminished to only a shadow of its former strength. Part of the decline was caused by artistic stagnation in the theater itself. American drama lagged twenty years behind the creative trends of other genres, and the current of realism did not touch the theater to any great extent until the war had revolutionized its social outlook, making the slick melodramas and romantic comedies produced by a generation of American playwrights seem naïve in comparison with the intellectual vitality of the work of a half-dozen European dramatists. By the time that the Little Theater movement had succeeded in Greenwich Village, most of the upstate houses were being converted to handle motion pictures, and the thirty- or forty-year history of practically all the Hudson River theaters had ended.

For as long as men have been coming to the Hudson they have thought in terms of what could be derived from this great river. Two hundred years ago its wealth was in its fish and its potential as an important transportation artery. Today we turn to the river for water to drink, power to turn generators, and vast recreational advantages that have not yet been fully explored.

The Hudson is not lordly or majestic. It seems never to change, and it is difficult to avoid the romantic trap of personifying it. The river is beautiful and beguiling, but its survival, unspoiled, now depends to a very large measure on the men who shape its future; they must remain civilized if it is to endure.

The *Leonardo da Vinci*

Stony Point, New York

"View of Storm King from Fort Putnam"
by John Frederick Kensett (1816–1872)
(The Metropolitan Museum of Art.
Gift of Mr. H. D. Babcock in memory of S. D. Babcock, 1907.)

Bannerman's Island arsenal
at the northern gateway to the Highlands

The Mohawk, not far west of the Hudson

The Adirondack Hudson near North River

THE SOURCE OF THE HUDSON.
IN THE INDIAN PASS, ADIRONDACKS

A print of the Hudson's source
(Adirondack Museum, Blue Mountain Lake, New York)

A print of the Brooklyn Bridge, May 24, 1883, by Currier & Ives
(*The Metropolitan Museum of Art.*
The Edward W. C. Arnold Collection
of New York Prints, Maps, and Pictures.
Bequest of Edward W. C. Arnold, 1954.)

The geometry of ice *(John Mylod)*

Three officers of these stranded steamers walk ashore for supplies. *(New York Public Library, New York City)*

View from 43rd Street of a water boy for the
Broadway Cable Car Company bringing refreshments to laborers
installing track in Longacre Square (now Times Square) in 1894
(Courtesy of The New York Historical Society, New York City)

A new building rising
in the New York University
complex in Manhattan

Office buildings seem to rest
atop the oval Battery,
which was once the first line
of defense for lower Manhattan.

The river and the residential skyline of Riverside Drive in Manhattan

Washington Square Mews, Greenwich Village, New York City

Manhattan's Central Park, playground and classroom

The computer-card look
of the State University
campus at Albany

(Left) The hall of a building on the State University campus at Albany

Fishkill's old Dutch church, where Enoch Crosby was temporarily held prisoner

St. Gregory's Episcopal Church in Woodstock, New York

A view north from the U.S. Military Academy toward Newburgh Bay

The North American Martyrs Church, Putnam Valley, New York

An Episcopal church in Cold Spring, New York

Broadway below City Hall Park was a challenge to navigate in the mid-1870s, especially at the Park Row intersection.
(Courtesy of The New York Historical Society, New York City)

Panoramic view of mid–nineteenth-century Manhattan
(*Courtesy of The New York Historical Society, New York City*)

The flagship of the U.S. Merchant Marine

Fueling for an Atlantic crossing at a North River pier

This ship is one of more than ten thousand
that clear the Port of New York each year.

"New York Bay and Harbor" by J. C. Wales
(The Metropolitan Museum of Art.
The Edward W. C. Arnold Collection of New York.
Prints, Maps, and Pictures. Bequest of Edward W. C. Arnold, 1954.)

Miss New York at the Battery takes on passengers for Staten Island.

The Brooklyn skyline spreads opposite Manhattan ferry slips.

Slips on the tip of Manhattan

Derricks in dock at an East River pier

A pier at the Fulton Fish Market, on the East River

Four views of the Mid-Hudson Bridge
at Poughkeepsie *(John Mylod)*

The freight bridge at Albany

Haying near Highland Mills, New York

Canapas Lake, Putnam Valley

Henry Hudson first visited Indian villages in this vicinity.

In the old days tracks 1 and 3 were used for westbound trains only, but a computer signal system has eliminated that tradition.

Commuter coaches in the Harmon, New York, yards

Along an Adirondack trail

Lumbering stages in diorama *(Adirondack Museum)*

The Hudson River is harnessed at Glens Falls, New York.

These piles of pulp wood will be pressed
into paper at a Ticonderoga, New York, mill.

Early road-builders in the Hudson Valley often followed crooked cow paths like those on this Dutchess County farm.

A rural mail-delivery route near Cold Spring, New York

The Neilson farm, now part of Saratoga National Historic Park

A house in Saratoga Springs

The Skidmore College library in Saratoga Springs

Main Street, Saratoga Springs

Drinking the mineral water at Saratoga
(*New York Public Library, New York City*)

The Colonial Van Cortlandt manor house

Boscobel's south front at Garrison-on-Hudson, New York

The old Warren County Clerk's office, Lake George Village, New York

The Vassar College library in Poughkeepsie *(John Mylod)*

Vassar's chapel *(John Mylod)*

Peter Bronck's barn in Greene County, built with many sides to disprove the superstitions of his slaves

Hudson, New York *(John Mylod)*

The tower at Olana, Hudson, New York *(John Mylod)*

The Schuyler house, Schuylerville, Saratoga County *(John Mylod)*

Washington Irving was understandably furious
when the Hudson River Railroad sliced off the waterfront
of his Sunnyside estate in Irvington, New York.

The ivy-covered east wall
of Washington Irving's study at Sunnyside

These grave markers have glistened
in the mid-morning sun for two hundred years.

"To the greater glory of God . . ." Missionary St. Isaac Jogues
was martyred by Mohawk Indians in 1646.
This memorial is near Lake George, New York.

Monument commemorating the Battle of Lake George in 1755

Rebel officers with Washington
as the Declaration of Independence is read in Manhattan

General Washington established his headquarters
here during the battles of White Plains.

General Washington bids his officers farewell at Fraunces's Tavern.

The
General Patton
statue
at West Point

A cannon guards the woods at Stony Point,
where Anthony Wayne recaptured the
American garrison in bloody hand-to-hand combat.

Officers' homes in West Point

"Liberty ships"

"Scene from the Battery with a Portrait of the Frigate Franklin, 74 Guns," by Thomas Thompson (1775–1852) *(The Metropolitan Museum of Art. The Edward W. C. Arnold Collection of New York Prints, Maps, and Pictures. Bequest of Edward W. C. Arnold, 1954.)*

Ships of the reserve fleet
ride at anchor
in the lee of the Dunderburg.

179

Fort Ticonderoga

"Lake George," an oil by John Frederick Kensett
(The Metropolitan Museum of Art.
Bequest of Maria DeWitt Jesup, 1915.)

181

Lake George at Bolton Landing

A beginner's skiing slope (minus snow) at Bear Mountain State Park

Public camp sites and picnic groves are expanded every season.

This Catskill playhouse is famous
for summer stock and experimental theater.

Entrance hall of the old Metropolitan Museum of Art
on 14th Street, painted by Frank Waller (1842–1923)
(The Metropolitan Museum of Art. Purchase, 1920.)

"Family of Deer" by Arthur F. Tait (1819–1905)
(The Metropolitan Museum of Art. Gift of Mrs. Darwin Morse, 1963.)

(Right) Wheeler Williams's "The Muse" in Sterling Forest, Tuxedo, N.Y.

"Fresh Eggs" by Winslow Homer
(*Collection of The Whitney Museum of American Art, New York.*
Gift of Mr. and Mrs. Arthur G. Altschul. Photo by Geoffrey Clements.)

Under the falls, Catskill Mountains, from a painting by Winslow Homer
(Courtesy of The New York Historical Society, New York City)

UNDER THE FALLS, CATSKILL MOUNTAINS.—[FROM A PAINTING BY WINSLOW HOMER.]

Holstein heifers awaiting their
hay quota on a Pleasant Valley farm *(John Mylod)*

The pockmarks of a January thaw *(John Mylod)*

This whitewashed fence keeps a farmer's road in place.

(Right) Central Park

Sterling Forest, Tuxedo

The shapes of Albany's urban renewal

The State Education Building, Albany

(Left and above) The State Capitol in Albany

Small-town scene

The Hudson is well over one hundred feet deep
in this section, below Ladycliff College.

This atomic-energy plant at Indian Point, New York, generates electricity for New York City.

The Water Level Route, a main line of the Penn Central

Engines in the Smith's Clove Museum at
Monroe, New York, commemorate the heyday of steam.

This type of locomotive was used on New York railroads during the 1890s. Here it waits on a Cold Spring siding for a scene in *Hello Dolly,* filmed in 1968 in Garrison, New York.

Batch plant on the Hudson at Yonkers, New York

Mile-long conveyers
carry aggregate
to Hudson River
cement plants from
quarries near Coxsackie.

Barges loaded with sand and gravel glide
past each other at the mouth of the Kill Van Kull.

Replaced by a permanent beacon at the mouth
of the Hudson, this lightship is now open
to the public at an East River pier.
(John Mylod)

"On the Hudson" by Thomas Doughty (1793–1856)
(*The Metropolitan Museum of Art. Gift of Samuel P. Avery, 1891.*)

"Mohawk Valley" by Alexander Helwig Wyant (1836–1892)
(*The Metropolitan Museum of Art.*
Gift of Mrs. George E. Schank, 1913,
in memory of Arthur Hoppock Hearn.)

Sculptured saints in a peaceful wooded
shrine near West Haverstraw, New York

Sterling Forest

Research center near Tuxedo, New York

The Van Cortlandt ferry house on the Croton River

A terraced kitchen-garden

The Seamen's Institute overlooking Battery Park on lower Manhattan

Broadway, south of Spring Street, in 1857:
a fire truck and the Young and Ward Omnibus Line

The Washington Square Arch at the foot of Fifth Avenue

The steps of the U.S. Treasury Building

Commodore Cornelius Vanderbilt (left foreground)
drives two fast trotters on Sunday afternoon
through upper Manhattan's Harlem Lane,
a popular bridle path left unpaved until the twentieth century.
(Courtesy of The New York Historical Society, New York City)

A nineteenth-century stagecoach on the lower West Side of Manhattan
(*Courtesy of The New York Historical Society, New York City*)

The Francis Skiddy, always a popular boat,
met tragedy when it rammed a sloop off Poughkeepsie.
(New York Public Library, New York City)

The Storm King Highway disappears in the trees
above the Day Line's *Alexander Hamilton*.

One modern oil barge can carry the same cargo
that once required a whole "tow."

Iona Island light

Raising the Erie Canal above sea level at Waterford

Barges prior to delivery

Water rushes down a stone alley
as one of the Erie locks is drained at Waterford.

Workmen begin repair operations on a pipeline to Governor's Island.

Governor's Island and the ferry are behind this small tow.

Even the rocks look forbidding at Sing Sing.

A tug guides a lone barge
toward a North River landing.

227

The Bear Mountain Bridge

Concrete piers in the middle of the Tappan Zee Bridge

The Spuyten Duyvil freight bridge swivels where the
Harlem and Hudson rivers meet at the northern tip of Manhattan.

The George Washington Bridge

Land taxes forced the west-shore division
of the Penn Central to become a one-track railroad.

BIBLIOGRAPHY

Ralph Aderman, ed. *The Letters of James Kirke Paulding*. Madison, Wisc.: 1962.

Bacon, Edgar Mayhew. *The Hudson River from Ocean to Source*. New York: 1902.

Barnes, P. R. *Crum Elbow Folks*. New York: 1938.

Barrus, Clara. *Whitman and Burroughs: Comrades*. New York: 1931.

Beam, Philip. *Winslow Homer at Prout's Neck*. Boston: 1966.

Bogardus, Mary. *Crisis in the Catskills*. New York: 1960.

Bowen, Croswell. *Great River of the Mountains: The Hudson*. New York: 1941.

Breslin, Howard. *Shad Run*. New York: 1953.

Brooks, Van Wyck. *The World of Washington Irving*. New York: 1944.

Brown, Henry Collins. *The Lordly Hudson*. New York: 1937.

Bruce, Wallace. *The Hudson*. New York: 1901.

Buckman, David Lear. *Old Steamboat Days on the Hudson River*. New York: 1907.

Burroughs, John. *John Burroughs' America*. New York: 1951.

Carmer, Carl. *The Hudson*. New York: 1939.

Chastellux, Marquis de. *Travels in North America*. Chapel Hill, N.C.: 1963.

Cooper, James Fenimore. *The Last of the Mohicans*. New York: 1951.

———. *Satanstoe*. Lincoln, Neb.: 1962.

———. *The Spy*. New York: 1946.

Daddow, J. E. *Study of the Speech of the Hudson River Valley.* Poughkeepsie: 1939.

Eberlein, Harold & Cortlandt Hubbard. *Historic Houses of the Hudson Valley.* New York: 1942.

Forman, Sidney. *West Point.* New York: 1950.

Goodrich, Lloyd. *Winslow Homer.* New York: 1944.

Goodwin, Maud Wilder. *Dutch and English on the Hudson.* New Haven: 1919.

H. A. Haring, ed. *The Slabsides Book of John Burroughs.* Boston: 1931.

Hill, Ralph Nading. *Sidewheeler Saga.* New York: 1953.

Hunt, F. *Letters About the Hudson.* New York: 1837.

Jamieson, Paul. *The Adirondack Reader.* New York: 1964.

Lewis, Jack. *The Hudson River.* Albany: 1964.

Lossing, Benson J. *The Hudson from the Wilderness to the Sea.* New York: 1866.

Robert Lumey, ed. *Juet's Journal.* Newark: 1959.

Morrison, John Harrison. *History of Steam Navigation.* New York: 1958.

Norsen, Irene Ward. *Ward Brothers, Champions of the World.* New York: 1958.

Reed, John. *The Hudson River Valley.* New York: 1960.

Reynolds, Helen Wilkinson. *Dutch Houses in the Hudson Valley Before 1776.* New York: 1965.

Ringwald, Donald C. *Hudson River Day Line.* Berkeley: 1965.

Scofield, Carlton. *Beside the Wide River.* Peekskill: 1962.

Sears, Clara. *Highlights of the Hudson River Artists.* Boston: 1947.

Shelton, F. W. *Up the River.* New York:. 1853.

Smith, Sandra. "The Whaling industry in Poughkeepsie," *Dutchess County Historical Society Year Book,* 41 (1956) , 40–56.

Springer, Walter. *The Hudson and Its Moods.* New York: 1929.

Verplanck, William & Moses W. Collyer. *The Sloops of the Hudson.* New York: 1908.

Whitman, Walt. *The Complete Writings of Walt Whitman.* Camden, N.J.: 1902.

———. *Specimen Days.* Camden, N.J.: 1902.

Wiltach, Paul. *Hudson River Landings.* Indianapolis: 1943.

INDEX

Note: Page numbers in boldface refer to illustrations.